BENEATH THE SKINS

BENEATH THE SKINS

The New Spirit And Politics
Of The Kink Community

by

Ivo Domínguez, Jr.

Daedalus Publishing Company
4470-107 Sunset Boulevard, Suite 375
Los Angeles, CA 90027 USA

Published by Daedalus Publishing Company, 4470-107 Sunset Boulevard, Suite 375, Los Angeles, CA 90027 USA.

Cover design by Don Mooring

ISBN 1-881943-06-2

Library of Congress Catalog Card Number: 94-71572

Printed in the United States of America

For my beloved, James Conrad Welch, who has been my North star, constant and true since we first loved on a chilly February night in 1979.

ACKNOWLEDGEMENTS

The many people who have touched my life all merit thanks in the development of this book, but there are some individuals that I would like to single out. I would like to thank my household: Jim Dickinson, Michael G. Smith, Nancy G. Stewart, and my lover Jim Welch for their support throughout the process, and for the brainstorming session that generated the title for this book. I am indebted to Eric Rofes for words of encouragement when they were most needed. I would also like to express my gratitude to Peri Jude Radecic for her example, for her devotion to hope, and for St. Jude. To Richard Labonte I offer thanks for his skill and delicacy in editing my first book. And lastly, a special thanks for Race Bannon for founding Daedalus Publishing Company, a much needed resource in our community.

TABLE OF CONTENTS

INTRODUCTION

This collection of essays is a snapshot of what I believe about the SM/Leather/Fetish community at a time of greatly accelerated social change. I write passionately about what I believe and it is my hope that you will not mistake my strong convictions for proselytizing. I am aware that I have many biases and blind spots and I am genuinely grateful when they are pointed out to me. I certainly discovered a few more in writing this book.

With the exception of a few instances where the topic or the theme was specific to a particular gender or orientation, this book was written to include the full range of gender and orientation in our community. Throughout, various terms are used to describe various communities, such as Kink, Queer, Les-Bi-Gay, Transgendered, SM/Leather/Fetish, and so on. Given that words have different meanings for different people and that the correctness or faddishness of terms is always in flux, I have used whatever words seemed appropriate. This is a book about ideas and essences, not styles and trends. I ask that you read for meaning, for what I intend, making whatever internal adjustments you need to make to fit your intellectual palate. We in the Kink community are diverse, with different political and ideological accents in our speech, but I believe we speak the same language.

I am a spiritual person, and I believe strongly in the essential health and rightness of my Kink sexuality. Many essays deal with matters of the spirit, and without compromising my own beliefs, I have attempted to frame spiritual matters within an interfaith and ecumenical context. I have also endeavored to make these discussions meaningful for and sensible to those people who are atheists or agnostics. Because my spirituality is an integral part of my being, it flavors even the most political or mundane essays. My sexuality is also an integral part of my being, so the fact that I am a Kinky Gay male is also apparent throughout the book. I make neither apology nor justification for either my spirituality or my sexuality in these writings. The essays are written with the validity of both those elements as a given truth. I speak from my own experience and have tried not to speak for others because I believe each individual and group must define itself. However, those insights or ideas that I believe are applicable to our community as a whole have been expressed as such.

My primary reason for writing these essays is to stimulate thought in the Kink community about the Kink community. Too often we are so busy responding to the demands or the attacks of the mainstream community that we forget ourselves. It doesn't matter to me whether you agree or disagree with the contents of *Beneath The Skins* so long as it makes you think. If it should spark a few lively conversations in your circle of friends and acquaintances then I shall consider it a success. Community is built one person at a time and one insight at a time. If we have the opportunity to meet, I hope you share your insights and ideas with me.

KINK AS ORIENTATION

There have always been Leather/SM/Fetish people, but it is only in the last several decades that greater openness and opportunities for sexual and social interaction have sparked the birth of a new community. As far as communities go, "several decades old" means that we just might be out of our childhood and headed for the turmoil of adolescence. This analogy is not completely accurate; individuals are not the same as communities, but some of the developmental stages may be similar. I believe we are at a point in the life of our community where we will test boundaries, determine the nature of our identities, our degree of autonomy, our values, and begin to set long term goals. This hard work to discover and/or to create who we are has not taken place in a vacuum. We are a diverse community with an equally diverse set of assets and liabilities. The Kink community is a composite of the different backgrounds overlapping in leatherspace. We are also a community existing within a larger culture hostile and disapproving of the sexuality at the heart of our community.

The view that *who* and *what* we are is a chosen lifestyle or a mental illness rather than an *orientation* hurts the Leather/SM/Fetish community in innumerable ways. For example, after years of contribution, without recognition or appreciation, the Leather/SM/Fetish community has begun to claim its place within the context of the Lesbian/Gay/Bi communities. We have raised funds for AIDS/HIV work and political struggles. We have provided committed volunteers for charitable organizations. We have painted the walls of community centers and swept the floors of meeting halls. Despite our efforts, we are still seen by the majority of the Les-Bi-Gay community as poor relatives they would prefer to hide, or as an albatross around their public relations neck. In fact, as we have worked harder for the Queer community we have become increasingly marginalized. We are subjected to a leatherphobia that is homophobia's first cousin. I do not like the terms homophobia or leatherphobia, but I will use them until better language emerges.

In the highly political climate of Queer culture we don't stand a chance of claiming our proper place (whatever that may be) or of developing a useful dialogue, until we can present a clear analysis of our sexuality and our politics. Our community is having a hard enough time dealing with issues of racism, sexism, age and disability, issues whose validity is a given, issues that have borne the scrutiny of fine minds for years, so it should be no surprise that Kink evokes a visceral response. The uneasy relationship between the Lesbian/Gay and the Bisexual communities is another indication that we need our own analysis of our sexuality and our politics. There may be many parallels between the growing awarenesses in the Bi movement and the Kink community's own awakenings. We in the Leather/SM/Fetish community may have strong feelings and intuitions about our essential rightness and our worth, not unlike Women, People of Color, and Gay/Lesbian people did in the earliest days of their movements, but until we can join those feelings to ideas and to spirit that can be shared with others, the possibilities for dialogue are limited.

In the face of the challenge of diversity and the antagonism of mainstream culture, the task of defining who we are is crucial to our progress. This means defining the nature of our sexualities, our tribes, and our community in a holistic manner that speaks to all levels of our personal and collective psyches. I recognize that the Leather/SM/Fetish community is composed of people of all colors, sexual orientations, gender identities, and other sources of identity, but as a Gay man I can only speak with assuredness about my own experience. In the examples that follow I do not mean to exclude anyone; my perspective is the field of vision of my two eyes, and I invite you to take my ideas and to run with them down the path of your own experiences. I see parallels between the evolution of Gay/Lesbian identity and the evolution of Leather/SM/Fetish identity. The Gay/Lesbian community over the course of this century has been working to change the way that its members and the world conceptualize homosexuality. Great strides have been made towards seeing homosexuality as a natural variation rather than as an illness. Dr. Alfred Kinsey's famous continuum and his studies created breathing room for individuals and researchers to explore human sexuality.

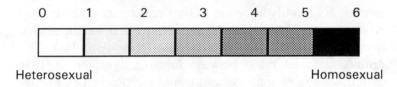

0   1   2   3   4   5   6

Heterosexual   Homosexual

The Kinsey Continuum
(Figure 1)

The concept of sexual orientation made it possible to see homosexuality as a deeply rooted part of self-identity rather than as a perverse choice. The Homosexual people became the Gay/Lesbian community as they began to define and redefine themselves, rejecting the mainstream culture's fears and prejudices. In addition to the emotional and psychological benefits that individuals have received from positive self-definition, over time the concept of orientation has led to legal grounds for considering Gay/Lesbian people as a class in the eyes of the law. This is one of the foundations of the struggle for Gay/Lesbian rights. As important as this may be, we must not forget that Queer struggles are about cultural change and sexual liberation—not just about civil rights, and certainly not about assimilation. For Kinky people, it should be very clear that

15

assimilation into mainstream culture is probably impossible and undesirable.

The belief that we are a people is also central to the web of connections that holds the Gay/Lesbian community together. It is my assessment that the Leather/SM/Fetish community could make significant advances in its health and standing as a community if it took on the task of defining Kink as an orientation. A logical outcome of this work would be greater clarity about the nature of our tribes, our community, and our sense of ourselves as a people. If I identify myself to people as Gay, Cuban, and Feminist I generally get responses that indicate that each of those three have told them something about my identity. If I identify myself as a Gay Leatherman, generally Gay is seen as a genuine part of my identity and Leatherman is relegated to the category of lifestyle or aberration. There is a distinction to be made between *labels* and *names*. A label diminishes people and reduces them to the stereotype or image that the label describes by pretending to accurately depict the contents of the person or thing labeled. A name expresses a facet of identity, and does not pretend to tell everything about the person or thing being named. Defining ourselves is a way of naming ourselves.

To make the leap to seeing Kink as a sexual orientation, some commonly held baggage must be left behind. The myth of Monosexuality is the most important. Monosexuality means different things to different people, for some it is the belief that everyone is really either gay or straight, and for others it means that human sexuality can be described as a continuum with heterosexual and homosexual as its poles. The essence of Monosexuality is that sexuality is mostly about whether you are attracted to your own gender, opposite gender, or both. I believe that an individual's sexuality is a complex pattern of many continuums, each describing an important part of the individual's sexuality.

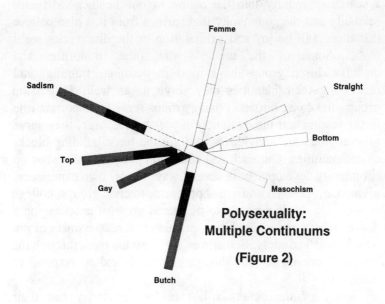

**Polysexuality:
Multiple Continuums

(Figure 2)**

This is Polysexuality, a concept that allows the Gay/Straight/Bi component of sexuality to be on an equal footing with the Leather/SM/Fetish component.

To make the leap towards creating a cultural and political analysis for our orientations, our tribes, and our community, we have to be willing to delve into ourselves to discover what is authentic and what is internalized leatherphobia. The mainstream culture is uncomfortable and ambivalent about sexuality, the human body, and power. Of one thing we can be sure—much of what the mainstream culture cannot cope with has been projected onto us. The question is how much have those projected shadows affected us, how will we let them go, and how will we make peace with what is genuine?

17

Endurance is a virtue that the Leather/SM/Fetish community values. I believe we will have the strength to endure the pain of a searching inquiry into the nature of our Leather/SM/Fetish sexuality and the community that springs from it. I also believe that there will be joy and exhilaration in the discoveries we'll make. Some of the methods that other minorities and disenfranchised groups have used in defining, framing, and reclaiming their identities may serve us as well. Discussion groups and consciousness raising groups serve an important role in the testing and the evolution of ideas. Moreover, they serve to strengthen the individuals who are the basic building blocks of communities. Outreach and education programs also spur on community development in several ways. In my own experience, giving Gay/Lesbian awareness programs to civic groups, college classes, etc. leads not only to the stated goals of encouraging a dialogue between communities, but also to a reassessment of my own beliefs and ideas. Sometimes we learn the most through the effort of organizing our thoughts to teach and to respond to questions.

Many of the beliefs still true for me today had their beginnings in the consciousness raising and discussion groups I attended as part of my coming out as a Gay man. I wish there had been similar groups for my second coming out, into Kink. Discussions about what constitutes Kink would be a good community building strategy. While hardly an exhaustive list, the five areas of power, SM, Bondage, Fetish, and Role/Scene could provide the starting points for Leather/SM/Fetish awareness programs, and for discussion topics for consciousness raising groups. The following are some of the ideas I've been working with that I believe merit exploration and refinement through group process:

Power

The exchange of authority, control, physical force or the offering and/or acceptance of dominance and/or submission are a part of most forms of Kink. The cultural norm that we are aspiring to has been summed up as "safe, sane, and consensual." What this phrase means in the context of a society with as many hang-ups about power and sexuality as ours remains to be seen.

SM

Causing or receiving intense physical, mental or emotional sensations or states of consciousness that lead to the satisfaction (often sexual) of strong needs and desires. Intense stimuli may also be a part of another activity that is not seen as primary. The intense stimuli may be experienced as raw pain or processed into other pleasurable or quasi-pleasurable sensations.

Bondage

The use of physical or mental restraints to exchange power and reach a variety of states of mind. Bondage can be an end in itself or an adjunct to other activities. Anything that delimits, restricts, or defines a movement, bodily function, or the potential for one can be considered bondage depending upon context.

Fetish

Erotic power is invested in an inanimate object (boots) or particular parts of an animate object such as parts of the human body (beards). The fetish is of itself a stimulus, usually sexual. An individual may have one or more fetishes, each having varying degrees of strength, inclusivity/exclusivity, and capacity for transfer of erotic power. Erotic power may also be invested in bodily functions (pissing).

Role/Scene

The power and stimulus is in the context and the setting of the activities. This may or may not involve props, toys, clothing, dungeons or other specialized rooms, etc. How planned or unplanned a role or scene may be, or how big a part it will be in play varies. The essence of role/scene is the investment of erotic power into specific cultural milieus.

Seeing Kink as a sexual orientation (among many) is essential to the progress of our communities. In addition to Kink as *orientation* providing a basis for dialogue with other communities, it can be the glue to hold us together. One of the outcomes of the increasing openness and growth of our community is increasing awareness of our differences, of our many tribes. These differences can seem extreme. Sometimes it seems that the people I meet, who are supposedly members of my community (Leather/SM/Fetish), are from another planet. Perhaps we can agree that Kink is the central sun that our planets revolve about. You may not agree with my ideas, but I hope you agree that we need to attend to the development of the Leather/SM/Fetish communities' analysis, politics, and cultural perspective. I believe that we are at a dangerous juncture in our history. They say that blood is thicker than water. I say leather is thicker than blood, and it is certainly thicker than my Kinsey number. In the hard struggles ahead with the religious right and other oppressors will we stand together in coalition or fall separately.

A SECOND COMING OUT
DOES THE METAPHOR APPLY?

My experience is that for most people the blossoming of their Kink sexuality happens significantly after the start of their sexual lives. It has been compared to the process of *coming out of the closet* that Les-Bi-Gay people experience. Many Queer leather people refer to claiming their Kink identity as their second coming out. It is logical that Queer folk should make that leap of association and broaden the idea of *coming out* to include Kink. It is human nature to try to make sense of situations by fitting new elements into existing patterns and perspectives. This frugal approach to the modeling of reality can result in significant savings of emotional and mental energy, but sometimes the off-the-rack model doesn't fit without alteration. So how suitable is the model of *coming out* to becoming a member of the Kink community?

There are strong congruences between being Queer and being Kinky in this society. Both sexualities are labeled deviant, destructive to society, unnatural. For the most part, Queer people and Kinky people are neither raised nor acculturated in their sexual communities, but become a part of them in their adult life or less commonly in their adolescence. This gives rise to a special sense of apartness and alienation that echoes the myth of the changeling or the ugly duckling. There is also a common experience of loneliness and isolation—the "I'm the only one in the universe" feeling. For people from certain religious backgrounds there is the fear of sin and retribution. Invariably as Queer or Kinky people become more *out*, there is also the risk and reality of rejection from people who are valued.

There are many parallels that can be drawn between the two communities, and indeed for people who are members of both, the differences in the coming out process seem slight indeed. The strong attractor of similar oppressions and a similar path for claiming identity and membership in a community may ultimately serve as a useful glue in maintaining the link between two distinct but intersecting communities. As politically expedient and advantageous as it may be to focus on the similarities between coming out as Queer and coming out as Kink, there are pitfalls if the differences are not understood, acknowledged, and celebrated. I have often heard mainstream-identified Les-Bi-Gay people use the argument "Really, we're just like straight people except that our partners are of the same sex. We're not so different..." I sincerely doubt that a Kinky person would be able to construct a coherent identity image, without incredible mental gymnastics after saying "Golly, we're just like you except for the titclamps, hot wax, paddles, fisting, chain cuffs (fill in your pleasure/pain). We're not so different..." In addition to the different beliefs in the development of a positive self-image, the strategies and rhetoric for achieving sexual liberation and political empowerment must be different for different sexual minorities. It is true that politics make strange bedfellows, but a Procrustean bed—I don't think so.

For the SM/Leather/Fetish communities there are three weighty pieces of baggage that can be inherited from the Queer community unless there is an effort to develop an indigenous perspective on the question of coming out. One is the myth of monosexuality; another is the sanctity of the closet with its accompanying co-closeted behavior; the third and perhaps the most dangerous is horizontal hostility. To be fair, these are problems that exist in their own unique forms in most minority or oppressed groups, and are not specific flaws of the Queer community. However, I do believe that the burgeoning Kink community is deriving much of its formative influence from the Queer community in the same sense that Lesbian culture received key ideas from the Women's movement in its first budding. Also, to be fair, I believe that the Kink community is benefiting dramatically from its association with the Queer community, and in the same way that Lesbian culture has enriched the Women's movement with new insights, I believe that ultimately the Kink community will produce new perspectives that will enliven the Queer community.

The myth of monosexuality can be summarized as the either/or dogma: people are either Gay or Straight. Anyone in between is either confused or passing through a phase. Bisexuality is not affirmed as a real or a desirable state of being. Given that the Kink community is composed of people covering the full range of the sexual spectrum, monosexuality is obviously a divisive belief. As a Gay man I've found that the diversity of sexual orientations at various Leather conferences I've attended has been incredibly educational and liberating. One of the ways that a monosexual perspective affects perceptions of Kinky sexuality is the denial of a broad continuum of equally valid ways of being Kinky. It also creates an atmosphere conducive to the casting of aspersions on people who are *Bi* in the sense of being equally able to enjoy vanilla and Kinky sex. It also helps to intensify the already overly stratified Top/Bottom distinction, and to limit explorations of ways to conceptualize the complex network of drives and characteristics that comprise Kink sexualities.

While I do believe that people need and deserve the opportunity to move through their coming out process at their own speed, in the Queer community and the Kink community the closet has acquired quasi-sacred status. Closeted people are often coddled and individuals and organizations often base their choices and actions in ways that are co-closeted, co-dependent. You may ask how, by definition, do the *closeted* have an impact on the *out*? To be clear, out and closeted mean different things to different people. Many who go to gatherings of Queer or Kinky people at bars, runs, homes, and so on, are out in the sense of having friends and partners, but may be deeply closeted in the sense of no self-disclosure to non-Kinky/Queer people or unresolved intense fears related to exposure. I have seen this manifest in leather clubs in the form of edicts that club colors not be worn at Pride events lest the closeted members' identities as Queer or Kinky be revealed by association as they tour on their bikes wearing their vests. I have seen discussion groups flop because of such extreme precautions about revealing the location of the meeting that discovery of the information was a deterrent to participation, precautions that were put in place to make it more comfortable for the closety people. Increased levels of comfort may be one of the long range benefits of a successful coming out process, but seeking comfort or supporting comfort is often as great an impediment to growth as the abuse of substances to achieve emotional anesthesia.

The intensity of debates and debacles related to *outing* in the Queer community shows that beliefs about outing can approach a fever pitch equivalent to religious fanaticism. The lack of temperance and balance in considering the personal and political consequences of outing point to an incomplete passage through the process of coming out into a stable identity. The paired reactions of attacking or protecting closeted people ignores the reality of the closet as a societally enforced trauma, and the closeted person as someone in need of healing. Ideally, coming out is seeking health, and recovery is a never-ending process. When the process of coming out is halted or when it does not include conscious efforts at rooting out internalized self-hatreds, there is always horizontal hostility. In other words, anger, fear, lowered self-esteem, mistrust, and other venoms are directed at those who belong to the same oppressed group rather than the sources of oppression. Although this form of self-abuse is common to virtually all minorities and disenfranchised groups, and is exhibited in forms as diverse as People of Color burning their own neighborhoods and the Queer media pretending objectivity by destructive coverage of activists, it is my contention that in the Queer community it is particularly toxic because its internalized poisons masquerade as attitudes rather than actions. I believe that the Kink community, as part of the continuing movement for human sexual liberation, has adopted not only some of the words and concepts for the coming out process from the Queer community, but also some of its flaws. One needs only to read the letters to the editor of a random sampling of SM/Leather/Fetish publications to see the evidence of horizontal hostility.

To achieve a healthy and appropriate form of the coming out process, which is really the process of creating identity and identifying with a community, the Kink community needs to develop its own sense of the process. Most movements for growth and liberation work to increase feelings of self-worth and pride in their members as one of the foundations for success. I grant that for the most part there is not a SM/Leather/Fetish movement per se, but I believe that one is developing and one of its first tasks should be to focus on the healing of its members. The Queer movement, of which I am a part, has been hampered by too little focus or energy on healing and personal development. Though legislative, political, and social activities are also needed, they are no substitute for inner work in an environment that respects limits but encourages movement beyond them.

As a starting point, I'd like to offer a seven-stage model that is my understanding of what the SM/Leather/Fetish coming out process looks like. As in any other model, it should not be viewed as a straight line, or a one-way street, but as a set of interlocking circles, a multilane highway with a cloverleaf. People move forwards, backwards, get lost, ask directions, and do not necessarily have the same destination in mind. For myself, I have found that awareness of being in a stage helps to remind me that I have choices and options. More awareness also allows for better support, with minimized meddling or enabling, when I offer help to others.

SM/Leather/Fetish Coming Out Process

1. *Stirrings*

Thoughts and images of SM/Leather/Fetish sexuality arise spontaneously, during sex, fantasies, and daily life. People experience arousal that they directly link to SM/Leather/Fetish sexuality. This may or may not involve a scene or Kinky sex; it may be purely an internal event. These people may find themselves acting on these stirrings in an involuntary, unprompted way when they engage in sexual activity or fantasy. These stirrings may peak and ebb many times. Depending upon the person and the intensity of the stirrings, various feelings will be evoked: excitement, fear, shame, lust, guilt, power, and so on. If the stirrings exceed a person's capacity to cope or to compartmentalize then they often move on to the next phase.

2. *Denial*

The stirrings cannot be tolerated so they are inhibited. The person consciously or unconsciously tries to push all images and sensations out of their awareness. Depending upon the person and the intensity of the stirrings, they may seek help through friends, clergy, or counselors to eliminate the SM/Leather/Fetish feelings and desires. The person may try to redirect the pressure of the repressed feelings by expressing leatherphobic opinions or in overly strong affirmations of "normal" sexuality. Denial generally results in confusion, emotional distress, irritability, and a lack of satisfaction in sex and other activities. The person may attempt to block the experience through the abuse of substances, by becoming a workaholic, through unbalanced religious or spiritual pursuits, or with other forms of escape.

3. *Threshold*

A point is reached where denial ceases to be effective and the person crosses a threshold that for them is symbolic of truly being a SM/Leather/Fetish person. This turning point may be a sexual experience, a night at a leather bar, attendance at a discussion group, an honest discussion with a friend, or any of a wide range of actions. What is important is that the person has begun to think of the stirrings as a genuine part of themselves rather than as a cyst to be excised. After the initial excitement the person may cross over that threshold back again to denial, but they have now had an experience that is intrinsically undeniable. The forms that attempts at denial now take on are different because the person must justify actual events. Each time that the person crosses over the threshold they accumulate experiences that eventually become powerful enough to take them to the next phase.

4. *Whole Hog*
The person gives themselves over to the process. In accordance with their tastes and preferences they visit the buffet of possibilities and eat their fill, sometimes more than their fill. Excessive behavior is not uncommon as they "make up for lost time". They seek out new friends and social circles and often withdraw to some degree from previous connections. They begin to learn the language, concepts, norms, and folkways of the particular Kink community they have joined. For many there is joy in finding companionship, fellowship, and a place to belong. The person often develops an idealized image of attributes and the standards of the Kink community. There is also generally a steadily growing discomfort as the nature of the oppression of the SM/Leather/Fetish communities becomes more evident. There may be anger, fear, and sometimes polarization or reaction against non-Kinky people. Many of the factors that had kept the person's SM/Leather/Fetish sexuality dormant or in denial now resurface with greater focus and intensity. As they collect experiences, they find growing conflict between their image of the Kink community and its reality. The combination of this dissonance and the weight of oppression may push them back to denial or on to the next phase.

27

5. *Fight Or Flight*

This is a crisis. The person fights for their identity or they flee from it. Often there is confusion and the person attempts both. There may be a geographical relocation or the break-up of relationships. There may be denial as well. The person must reconcile what *is* with who they are, and how they fit into their world. They must balance the accounts of the losses and gains generated by their new life as a member of the SM/Leather/Fetish communities. They must come to terms with their expectations and their associated rewards and disappointments. If stability is not found the person tends to cycle through the previous phases and is often prone to substance abuse or self-abuse. If the person finds a stable center point from which to survey life, they may begin to map out a future.

6. *Leather Persona*

The construction of an integrated self is the goal of this phase. All the various elements that make up the whole identity are compared, and values and goals are reviewed. A leather persona is created, a unique way of being a Kinky person, in part out of the person's essential self, and in part out of the life and the flavor of the community that they've adopted. Life goals directly related to being a Kinky person, such as relationships or accomplishments, are chosen. At this stage the person may seriously explore the distortions and internalized oppressions that relate to their sexuality. If they achieve clarity and perspective, and begin their healing process, they move on to the next stage.

7. *Homecoming*

The person experiences greater balance and integration between all their identities. They feel solidly connected to the Kink community with awareness of its flaws and its virtues. They feel that they are at home. They begin to develop a sense of responsibility towards the Kink community and act accordingly. Over time, as new experiences generate new

28

awarenesses, they may return to earlier stages to process the changes, but their conviction about the authenticity of their identity as a SM/Leather/Fetish person allows them to return to this stage more easily.

LEATHERPHOBIA

The concept of homophobia has spread rapidly in the last few years, and become a part of common knowledge in most industrialized nations. Having become a part of the pool of resource ideas that many may draw from, the essence of the concept has been used as the base for many others. The word *bi-phobia* to express fear, hatred, and oppression of Bisexuals has gained currency as the Bi movement has grown, and more people are now speaking of *leatherphobia*, a natural extension in the catalog of terms describing societal dysfunctions. Although I believe it a positive sign that members of the SM/Leather/Kink communities are using a term like leatherphobia that implies increasing consciousness of oppression, there is a danger that leatherphobia may become a watered-down buzz word. It may be the fate of all key words used in social change to deteriorate into verbiage, but it is tragic if too quick and too glib a use of a word should divert energy and focus away from developing an analysis of leatherphobia. As of yet, the SM/Leather/Fetish community does not have an extensive history or tradition of scholarship or inquiry into its own nature, so a conscious effort to cling to serious thought is imperative.

Homophobia is generally described as an irrational or exaggerated hatred and/or fear of homosexuals, and in its most clinical definition is a pathology. Many people when confronted with accusations of homophobia will respond that they are not homophobic, and in the narrow sense of the word their denials will be correct. They may be prejudiced, biased, bigoted, discriminatory—but not meet the clinical definition of homophobia. Some activists have been using the word *heterosexism* to stand for the whole family of individual and institutional attitudes, beliefs, and behaviors that result in the oppression of homosexual people. No doubt many other words

31

and concepts will arise to describe the experience of oppression, but words ending in *phobia* or *phobe* have caught the popular imagination. I have even heard a right-wing fundamentalist organizer call someone a *Christianphobe* during a heated exchange.

Contemplation of the essence encapsulated in words ending in *phobia* or *ism* reveals a complicated set of associations and interactions that reach from the innermost cores of individuals to the outermost political and cultural structures. I believe that in order to understand such a complex dynamic there must be a large number of individual contributions of insights to provide sufficient raw material for the refinement of the concepts of leatherphobia, and related words, that we will no doubt be coining in the years to come. In other words, I believe that a sturdy grasp of leatherphobia will not be handed down from an ivory tower—it must evolve from the community. To make that evolution possible, opportunities for discussion, debate, and consciousness raising must be fostered. By opportunities I don't just mean formal events such as discussion groups or conferences, because it is unlikely that a large percentage of the community will be interested in participating within that format. It is possible to create opportunities by changing the norms so as to allow or even encourage such interactions at informal gatherings and events of a primarily social character. Expectations and norms of behavior can be changed at the community level, HIV/AIDS education has proven this.

While it is important to develop our own unique perspective on the oppression and violence leveled against us, I believe that there is much to be learned from thoughtful consideration of the status of other sexual minorities. There is also much to be learned from the interactions between similar minorities. The uneasy relationship between the Lesbian/Gay community and the Bi community probably speaks volumes about the future of the relationship between the Queer community and the Kink community. The competitive relationship between the

Leatherphobia

African-American and the Latin-American communities may foreshadow ways in which the Kink community will be pitted against the Queer community through divide-and-conquer tactics. An examination of a variety of oppressed groups and liberation movements will show that there are also ways that people within any given group will express horizontal hostility towards people at different levels of consciousness or awareness.

Because of the incredible diversity of the Kink community, efforts at understanding and working through racism, sexism, classism, and all their kith and kin must be considered a part of the process of understanding leatherphobia itself. We cannot be united as a community without grappling with the dysfunctions that separate us. We cannot truly understand the specifics of leatherphobia without teasing out the variables and the co-factors of other oppressions. We also give up an important tool for social change if we neglect our responsibility to heal, to fight, and to make peace with the isms and phobias. Without this arduous journey, we will give up, lose, or never reach the *moral high ground*. For those who adhere to the teachings of Gandhi, Martin Luther King Jr., and other such teachers, the value of the power of moral force is understood. For those who crave action more than resistance, I'd like to point out that moral high ground provides a good vantage point for reconnaissance—and that it's harder to shoot up at someone. It is also important to seek the moral high ground for the sake of psychological health and emotional strength. One of the primary manifestations of leatherphobia is the assertion that SM/Leather/Fetish people are depraved, deviant, degenerate, diseased, debauched, and without a shred of moral fiber in their diets. So we must earn our morality and our moral high ground.

Morality is not the same as ethics. "Safe, Sane, & Consensual!" may make a good rallying cry for a variety of purposes, and is certainly an excellent summary of the rules of conduct for the Kinky community, and it may result in moral behavior. But of itself it is not a source of moral force. Morals

33

are beliefs or articles of faith derived from religion, philosophy, or personal experience, and as such are not easily changed by debate. Morals judge whether something is good, bad, healthy, unhealthy, etc. Morals are the foundation for basic values. Ultimately morality is about spirituality, and the inclusion of spirituality in the Queer and the Kink movements is essential to undergird the ethical and ideological structures of liberation. Unfortunately, spirituality must first get over the hurdles of rampant materialism and a confusion over the difference between religion and spirituality. The confusion is worsened by the vehement condemnation of Kink and Queer sexualities by the bulk of organized religion, and by supposedly progressive political analyses that are often devoid of, or hostile to, spirituality. Spirituality yields two important qualities, without which any community or movement is doomed: an unquenchable spark of self-worth and a willingness to self-sacrifice. I believe that leatherphobia can *best* (not only) be fathomed and charted by people who are in touch with that inner compass that senses what cannot be seen. That said, I also believe that liberation is like an ecology, with many ideological niches to be filled, and each member of the community has important contributions to make.

For the purpose of stimulating thought and discussion, I'm offering a few comparisons of homophobia and leatherphobia. Think about this short list, add to the list, and work variations of this list and your insights into conversations. One of the biggest ways we can make a difference against leatherphobia is by keeping it in sight and in the light of debate.

Homophobia/Leatherphobia
Comparing Classic Lines, Slurs, Attacks, Etc...

- *"Isn't that sick. Why would anyone want to do that?"*
  H The attraction between people of the same gender is seen as inexplicable and unnatural. Homosexuality is seen by many people as an illness, although it has been officially removed from

the list of pathologies used by mental health professionals.
L The arousal that people feel from intense physical experience (possibly pain), objects or context (fetish, uniform, scene), and/or restraints is seen as inexplicable and unnatural. SM/Leather/Fetish sexuality is seen as illness, and little progress has been made to alter this opinion.

* *"People like that discredit the movement/institution."*
H Lesbians and Gay men involved in unions, the peace movement, feminist organizations, religions, environmental groups, etc. are often the targets of emotional blackmail. For the greater good, Lesbians and Gay men are pressured to remain closeted and/or renounce their identity.
L Leather women and men involved in the Gay/Lesbian movement, feminist organizations, AIDS work, etc. are often the targets of emotional blackmail. For the greater good, Leather women and men are pressured to remain closeted and/or renounce their identity.

* *"They aren't capable of love and mature relationships."*
H Relationships between Gay people are viewed as intrinsically less valid, less profound, and less lasting. The patterns of heterosexual gender roles and values are imposed on homosexual relationships.
L Relationships between Leather people are viewed as intrinsically less valid, less profound, and less lasting. The patterns of heterosexual gender roles and values are imposed on Leather relationships.

* *"It's just a phase. All they need is a good _____."*
H They'll grow out of it. As soon as they find the right man/woman, etc.
L They'll grow out of it. As soon as they find the right man/woman, etc. Or, as soon as they are healed of _____.

- *"They're represented on the committee, what else do they want?"*

  H A token person is often used as proof that the issue of homophobia has been addressed. The person placed in this position walks the fine line between being a pioneer and/or a betrayer of themselves or their community.

  L Most of the token Kinky people I've seen have been in Queer organizational contexts where they are often asked to walk the fine line between allegiances to several communities. A strong indicator of leatherphobia and our community's invisibility is how little the tool of tokenism has been used against us.

- *"All they care about is sex."*

  H Gay men and Lesbians are seen as oversexed and predatory. In this age of HIV concerns, sex (even or especially safer sex) is suspect.

  L Leather women and men are seen as oversexed and predatory. In addition to HIV related concerns, Leather sexuality is seen as unsafe or excessively risky, or all consuming.

- *"What a waste!"*

  H Some heterosexual people, when they find Lesbians or Gay men attractive, devalue homosexuality with statements that imply that since Gay people are not available as potential partners to them, their sexuality is squandered.

  L Some people, when they find Leather women and men attractive, devalue Leather/SM with statements that imply that since Leather women and men are not available as potential partners to them, their sexuality is squandered.

- *"Why do they have to flaunt it?"*

  H Simple actions by Lesbians and Gay men such as hand-holding in public, wearing a pink triangle, talking about Gay related activities, etc. are seen as breaches of appropriate public behavior.

L Simple actions by Leather women and men such as wearing their leathers or club insignia, or talking about Leather-related activities, etc. are seen as breaches of appropriate public behavior.

- *"Their lives must be miserable. They can never be happy."*

  H This may be a self-fulfilling prophesy if people allow it to happen. It also plays on the very real stress of being Queer in this society.

  L This may be a self-fulfilling prophesy if people allow it to happen. It also plays on the very real stress of being Kinky in this society.

- *"They are a threat to the family and society."*

  H If Lesbian & Gay relationships are condoned then the family will break down, and with it society—or at least that's how the story goes. This statement implies that Queer people aren't part of families, can't create valid families, and are scapegoated for changes in family structure in society.

  L If Leather/SM becomes just another lifestyle, violence and the breakdown of society will follow—or at least that's how the story goes. Because of the relative invisibility of the Kink community the family question is less prominent than the accusation of chaotic or destructive behavior.

- *"They're not a real minority!"*

  H This can take many forms. It can be the assertion that sexual orientation is a perverse choice, or a curable illness. It can be the claim that only racial, ethnic, religious, or other societally approved subdivisions of identity are valid. Ultimately it is a dismissal of the integral nature of human sexuality and that culture and community also has its roots in sex, not just procreation.

  L Even many so-called progressives have been unable to

Beneath The Skins

take the cognitive leap to recognize sexually defined communities that are not based on the gender of partners but upon the spirit of the sexual exchange. The general public for the most part still considers SM/Leather/Fetish as pathology and summarily rejects claims to being a minority.

PRIDE DAY:
WHERE SHOULD WE BE?

Every June there are *Pride events* throughout the country which, depending on the local politics and organizers, are styled as Lesbian & Gay, or Lesbian, Gay, & Bisexual, Queer, or some combination, with the occasional addition of Transsexual or Transgendered. Additionally, there are Pride events convened for particular ethnic and racial minorities that are also sexual minorities. For a variety of reasons these events have also become a magnet for Kinky people of all sexual orientations. Pride marches, rallies, parades, block parties, and street fairs are a powerful cultural phenomena that both raise and then help to resolve important issues for the plexus of communities that intersect at these events. Pride events are also like a fishbowl. The people and actions contained within its sphere are magnified, but also distorted. They are observable by those on the outside, but viewed within an artificial environment. They are held in a world within a drop, pretending to a diversity that cannot be contained in a small bowl. Despite all the inadequacies of these events, they offer a treasure trove of images, situations and genuine experiences that can reveal much. Pride days and parades and our place in them continue to be an indicator for our sense of ourselves and our relationship to a variety of communities. Close observation, examination, and extrapolation of these events may yield some answers for the Kinky community, and more importantly new or reframed questions about the nature of sexuality and social ecology.

Is a Pride event a march or a parade; a rally or a fair; a celebration or an action? At any given event, regardless of the wording of the flyers and the news releases, there will be great diversity of opinion, and perhaps more importantly of expectations, among the participants and the observers of the event. Although I believe that diversity and variety are often the wellsprings of healthy growth, in this particular situation they also contribute to a lack of clarity. When we strain to make our mental eyes bring the blurry picture into sharp detail, the most frequent result is a headache. Let me give a few examples, and please bear with me—I am advisedly creating flat cartoon characters to reduce vast human possibilities to the scale of a few words.

In the seemingly random order of march queues, a group of leather-clad people are placed behind a conservative political organization dressed for success. A young couple, one sporting a padlocked collar, is approached by the media as they walk. A member of the conservative group looks on and mutters under their breath. What are they saying to themselves? Ahead of both groups, there is a contingent of queers for animal rights, looking back at both groups, appalled by the image and the politics of the leatherfolk and the conservatives. In front of the animal rights contingent there is a Lesbian mothers group, quietly, almost politely, shunning a woman in their midst they've discovered to be transgendered, and wondering why an animal rights group should even be in the march? Standing on the sidewalk, watching the contingents go by, is a man with carefully colored hair, wearing the fashion of the moment, and to the people of his rural community of origin—unmistakably queer. He is telling himself, "Why can't people dress properly. It's no wonder that we don't get any respect from the mainstream." Back on the lavender-striped route, a member of an in-your-face-F-you-deconstruct-this! contingent is feeling anger and ambivalence, unsure as to whether the greatest threat to liberation is from within or without after having been read the riot act for engaging in an unauthorized piece of street theater that grid-locked the march. Two of the people in the leather contingent are talking about post march activities, one is looking forward to stirring speeches and the other hopes the rally is short and sweet so the dance can begin. One is disheartened that the words of power and radicalization will fall on uninterested ears. The other doesn't understand why celebration and joy isn't seen as community building, emotional healing, and just as valuable as dreary speeches. A third person, a member of a backpatch club, is eavesdropping and wonders what will become of the brotherhood of leathermen as the old guard fades and is replaced by upstarts such as these. Everywhere in the march, in every contingent, every group, there are also those glowing with the raw vitality of being themselves in public. They smile, they feel the heat, they do not view the crowds with jaundiced or jaded eyes. Like children in love with the wonder of the world, they see beauty and possibility in all the expressions of queerness and liberation gathered together for the day.

Should we be surprised, amused, or demoralized by this tableau? I don't think so. We are, after all, members of the larger culture and community and heirs to its unrest and turbulence. We are also members of many specialized communities, each engaged in the pangs of birth, death, rebirth, adolescence, or a variety of developmental stages combining to produce our particular blend of turbulent change. It has been my experience that individuals and communities encounter intense, tumultuous experiences and emotions just before coming to significant insights and growth. Pride events and marches help to bring out those intense, pivotal awarenesses. As Kinky people we are no strangers to the power of a scene or psychodrama. Consider then the power of Pride events and marches as scenes, and the elements brought together in the crucible of a Pride event.

Sooner or later virtually all Pride event organizers have the discussion about whether SM/Leather/Fetish people should participate. In the most treacherous form, it becomes a question of *damage* control by limiting the visibility or the participation of Kinky people. As unpleasant an experience as this may be for all involved, I believe that it is enlightening, especially for Kinky people. Confrontation with prejudice from people that you

41

theoretically held as part of the *us* as opposed to *them* can be a great catalyst for the development and the refinement of Kink identity. In areas or events where this question has reportedly been put to rest there is always a new twist or a new wrinkle because of turnover in the organizers and emergent ideologies in the community. Wherever or however this conflict occurs it is a lesson, a test, and a rite of passage. Beyond the immediate concerns of the moment: "How will the SM/Leather/Fetish people participate?," a greater question is raised: "What is our vision of the common good?."

As noted earlier, a good part of the confusion and antagonism at Pride events may be a matter of differing expectations, but it is the belief that there is or that there should be a common vision that causes the most hardships. The belief in a self-evident common good or a common vision of liberation as a foundation for building community is about as productive as building on quicksand. We see different truths. It is the strident, "Don't they see!" or "How stupid" or worse yet the "They don't care" arising from this fallacious belief that engenders real obstacles to dialogue and peacemaking. It is true that there are many visions of liberation accepted or espoused by particular communities or sets within communities, but these are local visions, not regional or global, local in the sense of true for that locus of people. Vision is about place and space, and where we fix our gaze. Perhaps if we can agree where to meet and where to look, we can then begin to discuss what we see and what it means. In the meantime, when we are marching together we should consider allowing our gaze and our eye for beauty to sweep from the person next to us to the furthest landmark on the horizon.

Even before our eyes leave the confines of the SM/Leather/Fetish contingent the question of *us* and *them* arises, but in a different context. Who and what is *us*, where are the boundaries? In matters of race, ethnicity, religion, etc., the markers for who is a part of community are fairly clear

42

compared to the blur of the Kink community that has yet to resolve into a detailed picture. As we march do you feel identity with the people into SM and bondage, but not the fisters or uniform fetishists? Are the Bear clubs a part of the Leather community if they have backpatch clubs? How comfortable is a kinky person likely to be marching in the SM/Leather/Fetish contingent if they are not wearing any leather, a uniform, or other visibly kinky apparel? As we march does membership in a club or organization modify what *us* feels like? How does being unaffiliated or non-aligned flavor responses? How do our various isms and phobias play into our perception and our definition of *us*, not just our party line on what SM/Leather/ Fetish should be. How do you feel about men, women, trans-gendered people, different races, ethnicities, faiths, different orientations, etc.? How many points of connection and commonality must there be between yourself and another person before they become actual rather than abstract parts of your community? Which differences block the consensus of community or veto the vote of personal inclusion?

All of us are also diverse within the boundaries of our inner selves. I have always had a debate at each Pride event and march over which contingent I should march with. I suspect this is true for others as well. In the Les-Bi-Gay community the fact of split allegiances (perhaps better termed multiple allegiances) is a constant. I know a woman who, at one march, had four separate contingents that she not only felt affinity for but had helped to organize. In the end, she chose to march with the leather contingent because on that given day she felt more oppressed as a leather person than as a woman, a person of color, or as a resident of a state under Right wing attack. On another day, she might have made a different choice. A Pride event, like a microcosm of the world, requires forced choices based on the limits of time and energy. The choice I have usually made is to march wearing my leathers regardless of the contingent I've chosen. No matter which group you march with, you are still all

43

your identities, and a statement is made whether or not it is verbalized. When I march with a political organization wearing my leathers, I invariably have significant talks along the route, not all of them pleasant, with my non-leather colleagues. When a woman of color marches with the leather contingent she is still a woman of color with the full cultural impact that implies. The diverse nature of the Kink community and its youth as an organized and identifiable community create special tensions that could be harnessed for positive ends. To the degree that we are open and willing, we can teach and be taught in the special environment of a Pride event.

Multiple allegiances become particularly acute when we speak of sexual orientations. I consider my Kink sexuality to be co-equal with my Gay sexuality. I also believe that human liberation is only possible if it includes a movement for sexual liberation. Given this, the presence of Straight SM/Leather/ Fetish people at a primarily Queer Pride march makes exceedingly good sense in the same way that men marching with women for women's rights makes sense. It also makes sense because the Les-Bi-Gay Kink community is at this time generally more organized and more out than the straight Kink community. For Straight Kinky people who wish to be more public, Pride events are one of the few places available. I do not believe it any accident that the SM/Leather/Fetish community is at the forefront of dialogues, controversies, and actions to bridge the gaps between so many communities. The Lesbian/Gay community has taken the rainbow, in many forms, as one of its symbols to communicate diversity. Is not the Kink community more diverse in that it includes the full span of the sexual orientation spectrum, color, gender identity, class, the entire laundry list, and includes types and orders of sexual and affectional expression and orientation that are just now being conceptualized?

So here we are, a rainbow of possibilities (now stretching from infrared to ultraviolet) at a Pride event. Why *pride* rather

44

than some other concept? In the history of movements and communities of oppressed people the most prevalent side-effects of oppression are lowered self-worth and self-esteem. Motivation and power have their wellspring in honest pride and self-regard in both individuals and communities. The oppression, repression, and societal disapproval leveled against Kink is monumental, so the process of coming out into Kink is formidable. The development of pride in one's leather sexuality is usually a hard-fought struggle, so where else but a *Pride* event should we be? Where better to shed shame and to claim power than in broad daylight? Most of us felt a thrill when we donned our first leathers, or went to our first play party, or our first meeting. It's a heart-pounding, spine-like-a-run-on-a-xylophone tingling, butterflies-in-the-stomach-popping-out-of-their-cocoonsthrillthat isn't once in a lifetime but repeats every time we really free ourselves, a thrill, at Pride events, telling me I'd loosed some of the bindings, that blood was running back into a part of my soul that had been numbed.

Pride marches are a confluence of many communities, a river fed by many streams and tributaries, funneled into the narrow confines of a street until they become white-water rapids then spill onto the delta of the rally before rejoining the sea of everyday life. Following the metaphor, you may find as you proceed through the march that you identify with the water in all its wildness, or you may be the supporting structure of the raft, or the oar struggling for direction, or the focused knife-edge concentration of the pilot, or the laughter and bravado of the trusting passenger, or the solid resistance of the stone in the stream bed. The experience, whether that of a Pride event or the rapids, is never the same, always ephemeral, potentially life changing. Like the river, Pride events are more about the journey than they are about getting somewhere. What is accomplished is usually invisible except within the participants' hearts and minds. And like that river, these events work slowly to carve out a new landscape, a new place, for a new vision.

45

Art Imitates Life?
Realism In Erotic Fiction

Long before I had participated in my first scene, had acquired my first leathers and gear, or had even knowingly met a kinky person, I made my first contact with the Leather community through magazines and books I was able to purchase by mail or in visits to urban areas where stores carried the kinky material. Printed matter was my only contact with the Leather/SM/Fetish community for the first two or three years of my coming out into Leather, and I don't believe my experience is unusual. Claiming a sexual identity that is divergent from the mainstream is often a difficult and a risky proposition; exploring possibilities through the medium of the written word is often a prudent first contact. It is easier for a novice to find magazines than it is to find organizations, partners, and a place in the community, let alone acceptance. Though I can honestly say that I read every section in the magazines I purchased, the erotic stories were read and re-read. They brought new possibilities to my inner world of sexual fantasies, some of which eventually became expressed in life through sexual play with my partners, and some which most definitely did not.

Our community's erotic literature is arguably our most easily accessed portal of entry. It is also by its very nature a highly distorted, or perhaps stylized, view of our community's culture, beliefs, and practices. Should our erotic fiction accurately reflect our erotic lives? What are the benefits of realism in our fiction? Or are there costs? What are the plusses or minuses of fantasy? Who and what does our erotic literature serve? These are questions worth exploring. Before doing so, I want to say that I am not interested in engaging in debates about political correctness or the role of art in society or whether sexually explicit works may be considered art, craft, pornography, or erotica. I want to bring attention to the impact and the power of this type of literature in our community, share some of my observations, and hopefully entice you into making your own observations.

I believe that much of our erotic literature is unrealistic because it serves, through the magic of the mind's eye, to create scenes that are commonly unavailable. The unavailability may be a question of material resources—not many of us can afford a full-fledged dungeon. And those who can afford a dungeon may not wish the risk of exposure related to actually having it. Or the unrealistic components of a story may hinge on health concerns that those of us following the credo of safe, sane, and consensual choose not to practice. In some cases the story is an outlet for dark fantasies too brutal for the light of day. Some stories are set in time periods or settings that can only be reached through the willing suspension of disbelief or through choices that the person would not normally make in real life. These places and times that for some people are charged with great erotic power, such as the Wild West, Victorian England, prison, or a backwoods biker bar, find reinforcement and elaboration in erotic fiction.

Issues of practicality and wish-fulfillment aside, there may be another important reason why the short stories and novels that depict us are often not much like the actual lives or erotic play in the Leather/SM/Fetish community. Storytelling is a craft with fairly demanding limits and standards. Have you ever written down one of your sexual fantasies or attempted to relate one to a friend or lover? Think about one of your fantasies. Next time you are masturbating, making love, or having sex pay attention to your inner imagery, your fantasies. I haven't done scientific research on the topic, but I suspect that if we had a device that could directly record people's fantasies, what we would see would often be surreal, lacking in plot or continuity, and would be quite unrealistic. It is possible then that in part Leather/SM/Fetish fiction is actually an attempt to pour the truth of the community's fantasy life into the molds of characters, plot

48

lines, and the conventions of storytelling. Actual life events are also not well suited to direct conversion to forms of stories though they serve well as raw material. Stories are like honey; they are the concentrated essence of many flowers, many images, and many hours of life.

It is also probable that our fiction is skewed and distorted by the *butcher than thou* syndrome or the *heavier than thou* syndrome. Writers know that their writing is one of the ways they are judged by their community. All writers have, in varying degrees, a special attachment to the stories and the characters they've created, and if this is multiplied by the higher levels of reader/writer interaction common in a relatively small community such as ours, then the stories also become part of the personal image of the writer. Many years ago my lover and I owned an alternative bookstore that specialized in everything the mainstream stores did not carry. During our time as booksellers, we scheduled many book signings and author events. The writers of kinky fiction were treated quite differently than the other authors; they were presumed to be sexual virtuosos and received many *unique* offers. There is considerable social pressure on writers to produce erotica that reflects well on the writer. In the current competitive climate of our community this often becomes *butcher or heavier than thou* writings.

Shortly, after the publication of my first kinky story, a few friends and sexual partners commented that they'd enjoyed the story, but had expected something more intense. I responded that when I write fiction, it practically writes itself unless I try to interfere with its natural flow. For me, truly intense scenes are a gift that are part planning, part work, part luck, and part something that can't be named. Life and art resemble and imitate each other, and there is a craft to both. Our sexual scenes and our sexually explicit literature can be stilted or stylized depending upon the intent, motivation, and desires brought to play in their crafting. I suspect that when writings become the vehicle for more than telling the story, they easily fall prey to

49

Beneath The Skins

our flaws, sacred cows, and shibboleths as both individuals and communities. More than one scene or story has been ruined by attempts to emulate, to match, or to surpass standards of leather studliness that are as unrealistic as the emaciated waif look is as a standard for healthy body weight.

Should our erotic fiction accurately reflect our erotic lives? Yes and no are my best answers to that question. Realistic depictions of our sex lives, our relationships, our loves, lives, and losses would offer support and opportunities for insight to those standing at the threshold of our community, and to those at its heart. Such erotica would help us to reclaim the *actuality* of our loves and lives rather than the stereotypes we often embrace. I believe that there can be great healing through the use of stories that speak our truth, but all of our truth does not fit into the tidy box of realism. Rather, it extends into the realms of myth and fantasy. Stories limited strictly to the *realistic* are untrue, by omission, because our inner lives of fantasy, dream, archetype, and myth are emotionally and spiritually as real as anything we do in the physical world. Race Bannon has written of people having different *reality thresholds*, different needs for the presence or absence of props in sexual play to make it fulfill fantasies, or the degree to which an action must be carried out to be satisfying. The same is probably true for readers of erotic fiction, but with one important difference. Erotic fiction exists in a virtual reality, the reality of the imagination where the measure of the fiction is its capacity to evoke the look and the feel of stimulating and satisfying experiences. To create a community standard of vanilla SM porn would be about as productive as the so called cultural revolution in China.

There are compelling reasons for the SM/Leather/Fetish community to support freedom of expression, but without the counterbalance of an appropriate context the support of civil rights does not of itself result in liberation. For novices searching for a frame of reference for their experiences, the average piece of kinky fiction misrepresents the norms of our community. For outsiders, these misrepresentations have the potential to generate further misunderstanding or to serve as ammunition in ideological wars. This would not be as critical an issue were it not for the fact that our erotica tends to be our most public face. I believe that a viable solution to this problem has already been worked out by the many oppressed and disenfranchised communities that find themselves misrepresented in the mainstream media. Diverse and balanced depiction appears to be the healthiest remedy to distortion or defamation. The criticism, the medicine, that has been spooned out to the mainstream media should perhaps be tasted by our own media. Beyond a call for greater diversity in our erotic literature, the question should be asked whether or not something should be done to provide other points of access to our community so as to diminish the inflated impact of our erotica as a portal of entry. This is not to say that our erotica is not important; in fact, the underlying attitude that it isn't important is a significant problem.

To achieve an erotic literature that better serves the community there must first be a belief that it is a worthy endeavor in and of itself. It is common for writers to joke about writing porn (or romances) as a quick and dirty (pun intended) way to make money to allow for more serious work. Indeed, many writers use pen names to avoid connection with their erotic works, and generally omit them from bibliographies of their work. So long as it is the norm to consider erotic fiction as a medium incapable of supporting serious work or *real* art, it is unlikely that many writers will apply themselves to the creation of great erotic fiction. For sexual minorities in particular, erotic art in all forms is essential to the creation of a cultural and a personal context for sexuality. As a community the development of norms and aesthetics that place value on erotic fiction as a legitimate form of art would eventually create an atmosphere wherein more writers could and would create high quality erotic fiction. In addition to the direct benefits such a change would engender, the work of reframing our own norms and aesthetics,

Beneath The Skins

distinct from the mainstream culture's, moves us along in the work of becoming a community.

Life imitates art nearly as frequently as art imitates life. In the case of our community this interplay between images, fantasy, and physical expression is highlighted. Radical sexuality is, in part, about explorations of boundaries and the discovery of new possibilities as well as ancient patterns; it is a quest, and it is research. Erotic fiction can be like a thought experiment, a way to test and to model possibilities. Erotic fiction can be like dreaming, an important tool in processing our individual and communal sexualities. In traditional cultures, the griots, shamans, wise women, and healers knew the value and the power of stories to shape, to heal, and to perform magic. Life and art interpenetrate each other with active and passive roles as rich with ambiguity and purpose as two lovers' tongues and mouths engaged in the dance of a kiss. Our community plays with power. Why shouldn't we reclaim the power of art, the power of stories?

Butcher Than Thou

"Going out with your butch friends tonight?" a co-worker asked me, having noted that I'd brought my black leather gym bag and my vest to work. As a matter of fact, I was off to a club's banquet that evening, and the comment was just friendly small talk, but the word *butch* caught my attention. Not that I hadn't heard the word used a thousand times for a thousand purposes, but it seemed laden with meaning and dripping with innuendo. It might have been the look that I got from my co-worker as I zipped into my chaps, or the phase of the moon, or too much coffee that day, but the word butch kept buzzing in my head. It stuck with me like an infectious song or jingle, background music to my evening. Butch friends, butch talk, butch walk, and butch centerpieces on the banquet tables: I was tickled and appalled as I moved my way through an evening out with the boys. The next day I thanked my co-worker for triggering a sequence of perceptions that have served me well.

So what is meant by the word *butch* and where do we get the ideas that shape our concept of being butch? Is it a virtue to be butch? It does seem that butch is at the center of a constellation of traits and behaviors that are exalted by many in the SM/Leather/Fetish community. It has been equated with strength, solidity, confidence, self-assurance and other states of being that imply inner strength. Butch also has been taken to mean capable and knowledgeable in practical matters. This practicality can be expressed in splitting wood, changing the oil in a car, hanging drywall, knowing how to use tools, and generally just being handy. Butch also can mean the capacity to endure pain, to face hardship, or to look upon the harsh details of life with a knowing eye. So far so good as a standard of virtue, but it does break down quickly when examined more closely. Butch is also the word applied to behavior that is callous, insensitive, reckless, and ruthless. Butch is throwing the tools, slamming the drawers, and running the engine too hot. Butch is laughing at weakness, deriding empathy, and eliminating the competition. Butch is the wanton expression of the power and cruelty of a bully. Butch hates culture and refinement and would rather use art for toilet paper and statues for target practice. Butch does not believe in moderation and abuses food, sex, and substances. Butch is all the negative traits that this culture associates with the stereotypical male.

The Kink community, like most minority communities, is subjected to oppression and to systematic disempowerment. Those people who identify with being butch as a part of their character must walk a fine line to avoid identifying with the aggressor, the pattern of the oppressor. Currently, the oppressor is usually named as the White male with a variety of modifiers such as Anglo-Saxon, educated, Protestant, wealthy, temporarily able-bodied, neither young nor old, well connected, and so on. Truth be told, very few men meet the standard, although many derive privilege and benefit from those that do. Declaring an *open season* on White males, which has been common practice in some quarters, is no solution and is a form of emulating them, or more accurately, emulating the dysfunctional pattern that holds some of them in thrall. It is easier to be abusive than it is to be strong, especially if a belief in your strength and your essential worth has been undermined. The oppressed must be ever vigilant to avoid crossing the boundary between being strong and being abusive. Unfortunately, there are few role models of honest and healthy strength in our society in general and fewer still for people in the SM/Leather/Kink community. Being butch is about having and using power, about being strong. Of itself, power is neutral and derives meaning from context, so it is our intentions and our motivations that we must monitor and comprehend.

Part of the unhealthiness in our conceptions of what it means to be butch come from sexism and rigid sex roles. When butch is defined as not femme or not feminine, that calls into play all the misogyny and the resulting toxicity of our culture. Butch must not be sensitive, caring, graceful, nurturing, or any of the qualities traditionally associated with the feminine. Butch, viewed in this context, asserts self-value by denigrating and denying worth to everything that is not butch. Ironically, this perspective virtually guarantees that the person will not be able to achieve the inner strength and confidence that they seek. The concepts of butch and femme have been seriously distorted by the war between male and female. Some would argue that the concepts themselves should be abolished, but I believe that would be throwing the baby out with the bath water. Polarities and the continuums that lie between the poles have been a source of energy and vitality for humanity from time immemorial. Political or philosophical decrees will not alter the fact that arousal and satisfaction often can only come from the dynamism inherent in polarities and from a differential in power.

Maybe butch just needs to grow up. Most of the positive aspects of being butch can be separated from the negative aspects of being butch if sifted through the filter of adolescent versus adult behavior. An example of a juvenile butch behavior is the *butcher than thou* attitude with its accompanying atmosphere of rivalry that often detracts from the fellowship and camaraderie at gatherings of SM/Leather/Fetish people. Not unlike adolescents playing increasingly dangerous games to prove themselves, people playing at *butcher than thou* affect harsher demeanors and wear more extreme apparel to declare themselves worthy. The cost of this play acting is that even the person who wins the game loses because on some level they feel they are an impostor. The more vigorous the efforts to out-butch the rest, the more hollow the victory, and the more the distaste for the vanquished. The difference between *pretending* to be butch and *being* butch is the litmus test in this case.

The way that being butch or playing at being butch expresses itself varies with the gender and the orientation of the person.

For Queer men, being butch is something that the strictures of the society would forbid them. It has the potential to be an act of resistance and defiance. It is the cry of ain't I man too! It also can be capitulation and abasement before the ideals of a society that loathes them.

For Queer women, being butch is one of the cultural definitions of their queerness. It can be liberating to claim the strength and autonomy of being butch that turns deaf ears on society's insults. It can bar them from the wellsprings of womanly wisdom if it is seen in terms of either/or narrowness. It can foster a competitive desire to out-butch the men, an urge fraught with hazards.

For Straight men, being butch is striving for a cultural ideal. At its best, it is coming into mature strength, fullness and completion, but the worst is the more common manifestation. Acknowledging the feminine is healthy but to claim femme as a denial of butch to avoid the worst creates other ills. Claiming manhood is necessary for male mental and spiritual health.

For Straight women, being butch in this culture is a Promethean act, a stealing of the fire of power. It can revive many of the talents and the birthrights that were deadened by the blows of socialization. It can also be the trap of retribution and revenge if butch means adopting the ways of the oppressor.

There are many great lies that limit our lives and champion dysfunction. It is possible that the greatest of these lies is that you can only be one thing. We also see this lie in the myth of monosexuality and in the fixed top/bottom dichotomy. This lie dovetails nicely with the immature or the unhealthy mode of being butch. The combination goes something like this: you are only butch if every last outward detail proclaims that you are butch, and any evidence of being fluffy disqualifies you. This creates judgments and pronouncements that serve neither individuals nor the community. Perhaps you've heard comments like these:

"May look butch but I've seen the apartment, wicker

everywhere!"

"Looks hot, looks butch, but the minute the mouth opens it's a terrible disappointment."

"May seem butch, but wham when we were in bed—up went the helium heels."

"Sorry, I can't take that one seriously as a top, too short."

"I was the butchest one there, and that's not saying much."

"Oh please, you think they're butch, but have you seen them dance!"

This lie breeds resentment, low self-esteem and desperate attempts to become a caricature. Thankfully, there is a ready antidote to this lie, this toxic form of being butch, and it is humor, the kind of humor that laughs with and not at. It is the tickle and chuckle that bubble forth uncontrollably when you find yourself sitting at a banquet table whose centerpiece vase is a series of exhaust pipes filled with blood red flowers tastefully adorned with garlands of chains, spark plugs, and baby's breath. It is an appreciation for the humor and the beauty of the wildly unpredictable and often incongruous combinations of butch, femme and more that Kinky people routinely make, that can free us to be fully ourselves.

We must not forget the importance of being butch for Kinky people. We play with power, with the bleeding edge of radical sexuality, and with personal transformation. The positive aspects of being butch, the steadfastness, the steeliness, and the ardent passions are needed to shape the forces of a scene. Much of what is needed is power from within, which has few risks, but often effective SM/Leather/Fetish play hinges upon power over others. The power over others in the safe, sane, and consensual sex that is the community's ideal is a hedge against the risks of using power over others, but it is only a hedge. Bottom and top, or however else the power differential is being labeled, may give and receive permission to exercise physical or psychological control which certainly meets the consensual part of the equation, but what is the inner truth? Is the bottom being butch in the sense of the teenager playing chicken with a train or being butch as a warrior would in enduring an initiatory ordeal? Is the top hiding secret inadequacies behind the bravado of the butch bully or is the top journeying into the dark mysteries astride the mount of the bottom?

Appearances do not necessarily tell the tale in accessing the truth of a situation. Sometimes the most arousing, pleasurable, and/or cathartic elements of sexual play can involve imagery and action that are in the domain of the negative aspects of being butch. To the eyes of outsiders, many of the sexual practices of the SM/Leather/Fetish community appear unhealthy and unbalanced. It is the internal context of the sexual play that determines whether it is wholesome *and* safe, sane, and consensual. Attitude and intent are communicated verbally and non-verbally to create the context of sexual play. Like tribal peoples, we use masks, fetishes, ritualized gestures, and words of power in enacting the stories that give meaning and grounding to our identities. Unlike our tribal forbearers we have little exposure to meaningful rituals in daily life. We are even less practiced at the safe use of special masks and roles. It is easy to forget that the frightening masks and the fearsome roles that we wear during sexual play are not our true selves. It is also easy to forget that the masks and the roles are representative of forces and truths far greater than the individuals making use of them in their personal rites.

Heady stuff indeed, this discussion of the teleological nature of butchness, but the head isn't where *butch* is focused. Although intellectual understanding or analysis is important and should not be confused with truly knowing anything, especially sexuality, it is the response in our hearts and in our loins that is the touchstone for whether we are turned on by any given set of traits. There are prudish, anti-sex feminists, radical faeries espousing sissy fascism, and Leftist demagogues who would theorize or deconstruct *butch* out of existence, were it possible to do so. Sun Bear, a Chippewa medicine man whose teachings

I admire, said that he wasn't interested in philosophies that couldn't grow corn—that is, were grounded in the reality of filling human needs. In turn, I approach with great skepticism any system of belief that has no place for those things that feed the flames of passion. As a Gay man, one of the foundations of my personal sexual liberation was to trust my body's wisdom, not the external goad to compulsory heterosexuality. It would truly be taking a step backwards to deny my attraction to Kinky butch men and to feign interest in politically correct, sensitive new age guys. Liberation is about inclusion and that means the inclusion of desire as well.

Maybe the problem with the concept of butch is that it is a diluted descendant, a blurry likeness, a simulation of older paradigms of honor, of being a warrior, of being an adult, that have all but vanished from modern society. The full meaning of honor has been all but lost, generally equated with integrity and face and devoid of its original spiritual content. Warrior has been downgraded from champion of the people to a soldier wearing a white hat. Without rites of passage and transformation, we have few adults, fewer elders, and many adult children of our culture. The virtue of being butch in the Kink community is perhaps what is left, a reminder of greater possibilities. More than many other recently defined communities, the Kink community believes in the value of being or becoming a tribe and the benefits of ceremony and ritual. There are many seekers in the SM/Leather/Fetish community and if we are lucky they will pick up the clues and restore something of what has been lost.

"Going out with your butch friends tonight?" I've been asked that several more times since the first time it triggered a flood of ideas. Each time I hear it, I ponder what it means to the person asking the question. It has been small talk, a gesture of polite interest, a slightly demeaning jab, bait for a conversation, and the carrier for countless other messages. Each time I hear it, I ask myself what butch currently means to me, reminding myself

Beneath The Skins

of my own definitions. I also say a silent thanks to a co-worker for asking the right thing at the right time.

Marginalization Of The Erotic = Marginalization Of The Kink Community

Sexually defined communities can easily fall prey to the devaluation of the erotic in the mainstream culture, which results in a weakening of the bonds of community and of the perceived worth of both the communities and individuals. One way to refer to this devaluation is marginalization. The term has varied technical meanings in different fields of study but for the purpose of this discussion let's keep it close to the visual roots of its meaning. When the erotic is marginalized, it means that it is no more than a scribble in the margins of the book of life. The "margin" implies that the erotic is on the edge, and perhaps an afterthought, certainly not part of the main body of the text. The marginalization of the erotic also means that it is not at the core or at the center, and perhaps even that it has been cast out or banished. Center or core implies cohesion, balance, and importance, qualities denied to those things on the edge in a society based on hierarchy and duality. Many of us who are out as Kinky people may have worked hard to come to terms with our sexual identities, but that work generally does not result in freedom from the narrow view of the erotic held by the mainstream culture.

Let me give an example of marginalization at work—you've probably heard (or said) the old line that the only thing we have in common is sex, usually as an explanation of the relatively weak, tenuous connections holding us together as a community. This sentiment very clearly expresses the mainstream culture's erotophobia and illustrates how effectively the marginalization of sexuality works for maintaining oppression. Sex isn't everything, but it certainly is something, something very central to our

61

identities. That which is central or intrinsic affects every part of our lives. Being Kinky, especially if you are out, means a life history of making hard decisions about hiding, sharing, defending, and celebrating a devalued sexuality. Being Kinky means coping with oppression and both the anger and fear that come from the experience. Being Kinky is being more attentive to social cues, more aware of the masquerade of societal norms, and ever vigilant for the knowing smile that is the sign of a fellow traveler. Comparable life experiences and shared hardships are well known ingredients for building strong bonds of friendship and community, and Kinky people have a common store of both. But using the commonality of backgrounds and life ordeals as a foundation for community does not address the question of the marginalization of the erotic.

Sex isn't everything, but nothing is everything so that argument isn't very meaningful if viewed from a larger perspective. Sensibility, which in great part arises from sexuality, is a far reaching concept. A Gay friend, who I believe is now somewhere in the wilds of the Pacific Northwest, once lamented to me that he was concerned that as the movement for Queer liberation progressed and oppressions diminished, those traits that made Queer people special would vanish. He ascribed to the theory that *social stress, constraints, and emotional torture leads to sublimation of energy into creativity.* He also believed that much of the unique perspective of Queer people arose from their outsider status in society, which would be reduced as acceptance rose. Despite these misgivings he was anxious for social progress to occur. Similar assertions could be made about Kinky people. Indeed, the complaints that the SM/Leather/Fetish community has lost some of its magic because it has become more accessible and less secretive than in the past are linked to the same set of beliefs. In either case I would disagree, and I would also argue that this is a manifestation of the devaluation of the erotic.

These conclusions arise from the premise that sexuality itself is marginal and that the external interaction with societal oppression is more central, more meaningful. In a utopian world, completely free of bigotry, discrimination, and oppression, I believe there would be distinctive values and traits that would emerge from differences in sexual orientation and outlook. Those things that please us, that bring us pleasure and satisfaction, have an impact on our tastes and our values. For Kinky people, a finely tuned perception of power and force as erotic surely must flavor personal interactions, or at the least create awareness of potentials that modify the actual interaction. The Kink sensibility that can extend erotic power to symbols, objects, and roles, in addition to people, changes the basic relationship that the individual has to the environment. In this imaginary best of all possible worlds, I suspect that the forms of Kinky sex would be different but the essence would remain the same. If you or I were somehow transported to this place I believe that we would find the apparel and accouterments to be outlandish and perhaps humorous, but I also believe that we would recognize kindred spirits.

Society reduces the richness of sexuality in many ways in order to make it fit into the thin strip of the margin. One of the methods used is the maintenance of stiflingly restricted definitions of sexuality. Another is the creation of categories of valid or real sexuality versus invalid or unnatural sexuality. In this parochial scheme, only male dominant to female submissive, genitally focused penetrative, procreative sexual activity is desirable. There are many more limitations beyond these, but this is the main stricture. For Kinky people, though, this is just one of hundreds of possibilities. Further, a large number of the erotic practices of the Kink community are not genitally focused; some don't even involve the body. The importance of headspace, the inner experience of sexual encounters, which is so important to Kinky sex, is barely recognized. To recognize that inner, central, component would be an admission that sexuality isn't just a denizen of the outer, marginal world. The sexual practices of the Kink community are often marginalized by redefining them as violent or abusive acts, ignoring their inner meaning, or eros. Procreation is almost never a goal nor even a possibility during Kinky sex. The individual engages in Kinky sex for their own reasons and their own desires—not for the express benefit of the state or society. Though I believe that a fulfilled individual is more likely to be a productive member of their community, the current society only wants them fulfilled on certain terms.

Even in so-called progressive circles, sexuality is marginalized. The importance of sexuality is reduced to equations of economics, class oppression, and sexism. While all these are important, and the constructs of the nuclear family, the housewife, the institution of marriage, and countless others can be shown to be tools of oppression in the hands of a power elite, the actual value of human desire is not addressed. Once again the focus is on the oppression or on the utility of manipulating natural human drives and needs. In discussions with politically minded colleagues, I've found just as great a tendency towards nervous giggling and evasions when the topic has turned to sexuality as in any other group. Even in the presence of people who have expressed on numerous occasions the philosophy that all feelings are valid and should be treated as such, I find that libido and desire are still taboo. At its worst, the erotic becomes the pawn of an ideology. Desire is placed into categories of politically correct and incorrect with the expectation that true believers will amend their sexuality accordingly. If sexuality is central and integral to the self, it is unreasonable to assume that it is changeable by political decree, but pretense is possible.

In the SM/Leather/Fetish community it has been spoken of with some pride that we talk about sexuality with each other more frequently and more openly than virtually any other community. The societal sanctions against talking about sex are so strong that even other sexual minorities such as the Les-Bi-Gay community tend to be repressed in their dialogues. I believe that the nature of Kinky sex practices may have necessitated greater levels of communication if for no other reason than to ensure compatibility of interests and safety, but it is still a marginalized form of communication. Certainly more talk provides for more opportunities for individuals to engage in discussions of sexuality, but these discussions tend to be limited to surface appearances and specific acts. We in the Kink community tend to talk more openly about sex at social gatherings, and I certainly enjoy hearing stories as well as recounting my own, but this is still talking about what we *do* and not about *sex*. Although our style, as Kinky people, of communicating about sex is an improvement over the mainstream's, it still tends to be a variation on a theme rather than something closer to the radical truth. How often do people talk about what a scene or an encounter meant to them? How often has the transcendence or the bliss of an erotic experience been diminished by being described in paltry lines like, "That was great."

Sex and intimacy are closely related, perhaps inseparable. If that is so then how can sexuality be at the margin, on the edge, in the wasteland? There is also the trio of love, sex, and intimacy whose associations and relationships are all but obscured by the smoke and mirrors of conflicting realities and illusions. It has been said that love and sex should go together. It has been said that sex can be devoid of intimacy. It has been said that intimacy can be confused with sex or love. It should not be surprising that true communication about sexuality is rare when love, intimacy, and sex have been bound by shame masquerading as privacy and propriety. Nor should it be surprising that after sharing an intimate sexual experience many people are unable to express that intimacy. One of the costs of the marginalization of the erotic is an impoverishment of our vocabulary for intimate communication. Though the Kink community should not confuse quantity with quality in talking about sexuality, the fact that we are talking improves our chances of making a breakthrough in understanding and in communication.

The marginalization of the erotic in the Kink community also contributes to the disjointed nature of many lives. Certainly the closet exists for many reasons, but the belief that sexuality is a secondary or a tertiary matter facilitates the living of compartmentalized lives. While there are many practical choices to be made about when and where to disclose or to conceal matters of sexuality, the devaluation of the erotic tends to skew choices towards the living of double lives. If the erotic is thought of as not central to life, then it is possible to justify not sharing your sexuality with friends, family, and other people of consequence in your life. Since our sexualities *do* spring from deep within our core, the dissonance and incongruity generated by decisions based on society's falsehood produce suffering and disease.

One of the most important challenges for the Kink community is the reclaiming of sexuality as one of the primary upholders of the inner life, the spirit and the soul. As dwellers within the sphere of influence of the mainstream society, to a certain degree we willingly or unwillingly absorb and adopt its beliefs. When the mainstream society marginalizes sexuality it is pushing its own vanilla ideal to the margin. We must remember that we are far beyond vanilla and that what pushes vanilla to the margin may push us off the edge. To regain our balance as individuals and as a community we must reaffirm the central importance of sexuality in human affairs. We need to rediscover or to create anew a cultural context that values sexuality and grounds its importance in meaningful activities. There is a gravitational pull exerted between all things related by meaning in the psyche. As we begin to place things in the center, the rest will be drawn out of the marginal wasteland.

Art and folk art are two of the most direct ways that meaning and values are communicated and kept alive. The SM/Leather/Fetish community already has the beginnings of a rich and vital tradition of erotica. Whether or not that beginning becomes a force for healing and change will depend upon whether or not we marginalize our art and folk art. The work of Tom of Finland, Domino, Mark Chester and Robert Mapplethorpe, among others, has achieved some amount of notoriety and appreciation, but this is the exception and not the rule. Our literature may have a few fixed stars in its firmament like John Preston or Geoff Mains, but for the most part it has been severely limited. Our written art has been trapped by the belief held by many editors that erotica and serious writing don't mix or are not marketable. The venues for non-fiction written by our community for our community have been so few that the landmark books do not even fill one shelf. Our folk art is all but ignored. Where are the exhibits of club colors as folk art or the coffee table books of the art of the whip or other utilitarian tools that we ornament to express the flavor of our personalities and tribes?

A test of whether or not we consider ourselves worthy as a community, as a tribe is how many of us accord the study or exploration of our own nature the status of life work or life goal? Artists must dance with their muse or not dance at all, and for that I am thankful, otherwise we would have even less Kinky art than we do. Scholars, on the other hand, have much more choice in how they choose to invest their creative and intellectual energy. They also are more susceptible to the impact of marginalization because scholarship is a collective activity requiring colleagues and peers—a difficult thing to manage without the magnet of value. The work of the scholar complements the work of the artist in reinvesting power, value, and centrality to Kinky sexuality because beauty and reason speak to different parts of the self. The work of the researcher/scholar, also has the potential to have a compelling impact on mainstream culture because law and policy derive much of their validity from *evidence*, one of the benchmarks for truth in modern society. Challenging and changing the archaic laws and the diagnoses of mental illness that oppress Kinky people requires a cadre of our own experts. Where are *our* professionals? Most of them don't exist yet. They are not *our* professionals until they consider their sexuality, their kinkiness, to be a part of their core identity. SM/Leather/Fetish events and gatherings are often filled with highly qualified and respected practitioners from a wide range of fields. Despite the apparent presence of these professionals in our community, there is almost no presence of the Kink community in professional journals or conferences. While this is understandable when viewed in terms of the closet and career plans, understanding does not resolve the question of the damage and of the lost opportunities produced by those choices. There is also very little response to efforts to bring together professionals in the relatively safe confines of the Kink community. There has been a significant and honorable response to the AIDS/HIV epidemic by the full spectrum of people that make up our community. This is necessary and noble work, but it is its own work and not a substitute for the toil of creating an identifiable Kink perspective and sensitivity in the various professional communities.

One sure sign of the convergence of art, science, spirituality, the political and the personal that will mark progress away from the exile of the margin is the creation of Kink Studies. When we have coalesced enough as a community to support and to justify a curriculum on par with those of Women's Studies or African-American Studies programs, we will have come a long way. For such programs to exist, a community must have a significant number of individuals that believe in the worth of their identity enough to invest a considerable amount of time, money, reputation, and heart. By no means do I want to suggest that these programs or that academia are the key to reducing the marginalization of the erotic, only that they are important markers and tools. The real work is always deep within each individual.

One of the ways that that personal work can begin is through increasing awareness that sexual encounters are a deep form of communication. Styles and preferences in communication vary as wildly as do tastes in Kink. But, centering some attention on saying what you mean and meaning what you say before, during, or after a scene will eventually result in more conscious awareness of the magic exchanged in sexual expression. Deep communication is intimacy and offering the silence to listen. Although all sexualities offer this potential of deep sharing, SM/Leather/Fetish sexual expression is often laden with messages meant for more than just the parties involved. In our sexual play we often speak through our actions to our own personal history, our culture, our families, our world, and sometimes to our concept of the Divine. Perhaps fear of responsibility prevents us from listening too closely, because knowledge becomes power and hence obligation. Perhaps marginalization is a defense, the marginal can be ignored. If this fear can be conquered, or the disempowerment healed, then SM/Leather/Fetish sexuality can become a source of communion and an affirmation of living that synthesizes pleasure and pain, the severe and the mild.

If we are to be successful as a tribe, a community, in reclaiming the ground of our being, we will need scouts to find the way home. They may be artists or scholars of vision. No doubt we will need planners and organizers and people in all the other valid roles in a healthy community. What I believe we need most is *anchors*. There need to be people who claim their Kink identity as their primary identity and immerse themselves in the life of the community—the anchors. Because we have been devalued by the mainstream community, we in turn often devalue or belittle those people who have placed their Kink at the center of their lives. Those tireless individuals who put out newsletters, put on great social events, sell raffle tickets, attend long and dreary meetings are not wasting their time on a hobby. They are expressing a personal truth. The great diversity of our community brings to mind the image of an immense flotilla of ships of every type. When buffeted by storms, each ship must have an anchor to drop or they will be scattered by the storm, some of them lost. When the Kink community is buffeted by political attacks and oppression we too need our anchors, and respect is due to those that labor for themselves and on our behalf. I believe that sexuality will someday leave the margin and take its central home once more, but that will be a long time coming. As a sexual minority, the Kink community has many reasons to find its way home sooner than the mainstream. If we find our way, and I hope that we do, we must remember that staying at the center will not be easy, just very worthwhile.

Three Gay Male Archetypes: Drag Queen, Leatherman, Teacher/Priest

A number of years ago I attended a ritual that touched a deep part of my psyche, and stirred something in me that had been slumbering. The ritual, in the fashion of so many open circles offered at Neo-Pagan gatherings, had been hastily cobbled together with the roles and parts doled out to whomever was willing. Despite all the rough edges and all the nervous tittering, there was a raw sincerity shining through the ritual, obscuring the defects and warming the soul. Though I knew I was at a very mundane camp ground used for high school band camps, motorcycle club runs, weight loss camps, and now a gathering of witches, I also knew that I was on sacred ground. I stood holding hands in a circle with about 40 people, women, men, and teenagers of various sexual orientations, all drawn together to experience something of the mysteries of gay male sexuality.

This is not an essay on ritual or magic so I'll not elaborate on all the details of the ceremony. The culmination involved the calling of the triune form of the Gay God as the Drag Queen, the Leatherman, and the Teacher/Priest into the bodies of three Gay men in the circle. The shift I observed in their poise and bearing was unmistakable. They each addressed the group, explaining something of their attributes and their essences as aspects of the Shining Ones. After speaking, they each passed a symbol representative of their being around the circle so that we could feel their energy. The Drag Queen took off his wig, the Leatherman took a chain from his boot, and the Teacher/Priest offered a wand fresh cut from a tree, still bearing leaves. These three objects were passed from person to person with the deliberate reverence you'd associate with a tea ceremony.

Then the real magic happened. Throughout the circle people were sighing, laughing, gasping, some close to tears as they allowed themselves to capture a sense of the beauty, the wisdom, the poignancy, and the mirth of three powerful archetypes.[1] Most of the Gay men in the group were having compelling recognitions and remembrances of different faces, different facets of their lives. Many of the women and the men of other orientations were experiencing sexual otherness in a way that was intimate, and safe. There were a few people for whom the merest touch of each object was an ordeal. To the credit of these participants, every one of them held each. The wig, the chain, and the wand were returned to the Drag Queen, the Leatherman, and the Teacher/Priest, who then thanked the three archetypes and bid them adieu. The quality of light and sound had changed in the circle, the three presences were gone, and the three men were no longer larger than life. The circle was opened, the ceremony ended, and amidst the post-ritual hugs and merry-making, the leatherman was wearing the wig, the teacher/priest was wearing the chain, and the drag queen was playing fairy godmother with the wand. Afterwards the participants discussed the ritual and had a lively, friendly dialogue about the full range of human sexuality.

What awakened in me that day was a change as subtle, as sure, and as irrevocable as puberty. As with the turning of the seasons, there were not specific days that I could say were the boundaries between one awareness and another any more than you can say that yesterday was Spring and tomorrow is Summer. More exactly, you can say it but the weather will prove you foolish and arbitrary. The change that was wrought in me was the gift of seeing the divine within the men I played with, loved with, fought with. Indeed, as a Wiccan the teachings I held as

---

1/ In the work of Carl Jung, an archetype is a primordial icon, arising from the collective unconscious. It is an image, a symbol, a myth of extraordinary power that has a life of its own.

true said that all humans are God and Goddess incarnate, but having seen three faces of the Queer God, I could recognize this truth in the faces of my brethren. As with all core beliefs, this change in awareness began to cause corollary changes in my perceptions and my actions that permeated many areas of my life. Having studied my responses to this awakening, I am led to believe that a recognition of the archetypes specific to your identity stimulates profound healing. How this recognition is to be accomplished will be different for each individual, since it will have to mesh with whatever configuration their religion, spirituality, and philosophy have taken. If you are not a religious or a spiritual person, I believe that you may find that the psychological and the sociological impact of archetypes are well worth your study.

Sadly, oppression exists on every level, not just the physical or the social. For many minority groups, sexual minorities in particular, the archetypes have been driven deep underground. Knowledge of these archetypes has been all but obliterated from common knowledge. In addition to reclaiming or rediscovering the old archetypes, we are called to explorations of the present. There are new archetypes, or modifications of old ones, that are just now acquiring strength and focus with the flowering of new tribes, new communities, new peoples. I'd like to share some of my observations of three Gay male archetypes. For Gay men these ideas may have immediate personal utility, and I suspect for Bi men much will be applicable with some adjustment or amplification. For all my other sisters and brothers, the telling of this story may act as an impetus to seek your own lost archetypes, and may provide useful clues.

Drag Queen

He is a divine Androgyne, a blending of male and female energies, but also a trickster, a being who plucks truth and beauty from the jaws of chaos through guile and humor. He shows us that reality and illusion are siblings. He weaves a spiral dance through the veils of truth and fiction, flirting with both. On the surface he is a woman, one layer deeper he is physically a man, deeper still are layers upon layers of alternating polarities surrounding a center that is the mother and father of both realities and illusions. The power of the mask, of the role, is both exalted and ridiculed. He can be unearthly beauty without compare, and ugliness without measure. The Drag Queen is both the Bright Mother and the Dark Mother wielding the sword of High Camp. He is the anger of the oppressed, expressed through wit and charm and a slashing ferocity that knows where it hurts. He is also glamour tripping the light fantastic, dancing on the bright thin, interface between male and female. He knows about somewhere over the rainbow, and he can *be* the witches of North and South or East and West. He awaits us at the Gate of Dreaming with sand and fairy dust in his hand.

In life, embodied within the many, the Drag Queen provides Gay men with the knowledge that the fads, the fashions, and the foibles of society are ephemeral. With that knowledge comes the freedom to play and to create, like a Goddess before the wide canvas of the universe. But a little knowledge is a dangerous thing. If the Drag Queen's whispered truth is not fully accepted or understood then it is possible to become trapped by the glitter that is then mistaken for gold. The Drag Queen, whose highest form bears the heart of Alchemical gold, may become blinkered by the leaden limits of society's oppressive weight. He/she may in a moment of despair pawn the heart of gold for some defense, some refuge, from the ugliness of society. It is no wonder that the Drag Queen can be a love goddess bearing the nectar of joy or a harpy armed with venomous stings. There are many quests, many a storyline the archetype of the Drag Queen can put into motion, but I believe the chief one is about the union of male and female essences that lie beyond and beneath the fabric of daily life.

Leatherman

He is the wild man. The animal powers course through his being. He is both hunter and hunted, honoring the cost of life. He wears animal skins as a shaman, as a lycanthrope. He marks his territory with piss, with cum, with the red welt of his whip. He locks horns in struggles as filled with strength as with frailty. He is the irrepressible force of Eros and the sour sweat stink of panic offered as incense to a universe too vast to be comprehended. He is the dark joys and the absolute necessities of nature. He is a Lord of air and darkness calling forth the dreams and desires that lurk in the deepest chasms of the soul. He is also the flame that draws the moths to transcendence, then returns them to the mortal coil of bondage. He too is a paradox, both slave and master to desire, to authority, and to responsibility. With his strop, he hones the knife's edge that free will dances upon. In cycles more erratic but as real as those of the moon, he bleeds a sacrifice of his life force to his lovers and his tribe. He is also the Greenman, John Barleycorn, who dies to feed the people who in turn vouchsafe his rebirth. He sits at the feet of the dragons, guarding the gate to the Underworld, a thorny rose clenched in his fist.

In life, embodied within the many, the Leatherman provides Gay men with the mystery of power, death and rebirth. Desire, and its objects, are borne from the unfathomed depths within and rise to the light of day to seek satiety which is destruction. The death of desire is followed by its rebirth, and the cycle of the raw power of life continues. For the Leatherman who sees this cycle as the spiral of evolution gaining insight and depth, there is an expansion of the self that can delve deeper and fly higher. For the Leatherman who is lost in the materialism of the mainstream culture, the cycle is not the love play of spirit and matter, but is a vicious circle, a ball and chain, and a collapse of values resulting in spiritual sterility. Those who are lost become the demonic stereotype of cruelty, violence, self-abasement, and

jealousy that is not the Sex Magick of SM, but the sadomasoch-
ism of pathology. There is a grandeur in nature that cannot be
described by pleasure or pain, can only be their union. The
Leatherman in his highest form achieves the ecstasy that
reconciles the mercy and the severity of existence wherein chaos,
order, grace and entropy are honored equals at the round table
of eternity.

Teacher/Priest

Father to no one so father to all, he lives for the life of his
people. He is gentle comfort, reassurance and conscience to all
his people. He barters the little love of the individual for the
large love of the whole. The stories, the songs, the codes of law,
the codes of the heart, and the gossip flow through him and from
him. He guides the toddling first steps and upholds the doddering
last steps. He joins the hands of the lovers and lights the lamp of
wonder in the student's eye. He calls upon the great powers that
spring from the vasty deeps to oversee and overlight the passages
of life. He is the steward of the many colors, the many skeins,
that are woven into the rough homespun of daily life and the
treasured silk of the perfect moment. He remembers so that what
was does not become tangled with what *will be*. He re-members
so that the members of his community will not forget their body
politic. Always and always, he makes his sacrifice of himself to
himself for the greater good, for the group soul. Bearing a torch,
he lifts the veil to reveal the Gate to the Upperworld, knowing
he may not pass while holding the Gate for others.

In life, embodied within the many, the Teacher/Priest
provides Gay men with grounding and purpose in the weave of
community. He is freed from the fetters of lineage, of the family
tree, but bound tight to the fate of his people and to his children
of the heart. He is the friend who listens, holds up the mirror of
personal truth, and offers true counsel regardless of the temporal
consequences. The Teacher/Priest recognizes the value of the

individual within the context of the collective. From the lofty heights of the mountains of faith in religion, philosophy or ideology the Teacher/Priest can see the lay of the land and the flow of the river of time. When healthy and balanced, he is the messenger between the personal and the collective, an aspect of the rainbow bridge and Hermes. In the thin air of the heights, of continual consciousness-raising, he may become giddy, delusional, intoxicated with the vision. From the heights the promised land can be seen but not reached. From the heights the individual is reduced to an ant, insignificant in the landscape. The Teacher/Priest can become the ensnarer, the hound of dogma that nips at the heels of all who stray from the herd. Unbalanced, he can be the shepherd so entranced by the distant vision of the promised land that he leads the herd over the cliffs to destruction. In his truest form he is the bridge and the principle of agency.

These descriptions are just pale indications of the three archetypes with about as much detail as quick sketches on a mist-clouded bathroom mirror. But like those sketches, the gist is communicated and when the mist clears, the eyes reflected in the mirror will show a fuller story. Archetypes are neither words nor individuals but like them can be brought together in many ways to create new ideas. Like words and like people, archetypes change and are changed by interaction with and exposure to the world through changing denotations and connotations. Several archetypes may be in play having an impact on a situation or a personality at any given time. Although each of these archetypes is worthy of exhaustive exploration, I will narrow the focus primarily to the Leatherman and to the personal response to this archetype.

At the sight of your beloved, perhaps you have felt your heart tremble as if they held it in their hand. Or possibly you've found your thoughts circling round and round a vision of lust, binding you so fully that in days past they would have said you were bespelled. During an especially good sexual encounter, you

Beneath The Skins

may have found that all of reality shrank to just the realm of your senses and that time held no sway over your consciousness. Once in a great while, my partners have become more than themselves; they have been the God—or at least were the instruments of a higher force. I believe that when conditions are right, whether by design, accident, or fate, the archetypes are summoned and imbue our actions and experiences with numinous power. I grant that much of the richness of love and lust arises from the body, the mind, and the heart—but the spirit must not be forgotten. When the archetypes, the Gods and Goddesses, come into the bedroom or the dungeon, we should take note because we are changed by the meeting in ways that only spirit can accomplish. The changes are like those that awakened in me the day of the ritual of the Drag Queen, Leatherman, and Teacher/Priest. The changes are as subtle, as sure, and as irrevocable as puberty, as aging, as coming out.

The bright flare of sex is not the only light that awakens the archetypes within us. There have been moments filled with a dreamy warmth like a lover's embrace when I have looked upon a throng of leathermen at a bar, at a meeting, on a run, and I have seen each of them glowing with an inner light. On rarer occasions it has been less an inner light and more, a cloak that magnified what was present in the individual. During these moments, these reveries, people that I don't like, don't find attractive, or don't even have a shred of patience for become lovable, respected, and at times awe-inspiring. Seeing the Leatherman archetype embodied in the men of my community has on several occasions served me as an antidote to toxic thoughts and attitudes. Negativity, pessimism, despair, and plain old garden variety disgust are among the poisons that respond well to spiritual medicine.

A number of religions and philosophies teach that the divine is present in each person and it could be argued that recognition of this truth should be enough. In my experience it is not. On a psychological and emotional level it is important for the divine

78

or the spiritual to be clothed in a manner fitting to the individual and the situation. I believe that for Kinky people, having access to images of Kinky archetypes or Kinky deity forms is almost indispensable in order to integrate their sexuality with their spirituality. To acknowledge the divine within the self, to acknowledge a family resemblance to the Great Ones, requires that there be substantial points of commonality and connection between the individual and the archetype. In principle this realization and its corresponding actions are akin to the movement in the Women's community to reclaim and revive the Goddess. It is also akin to the efforts among People of Color to remind the world that divinity comes in all colors, and that many if not most of the founders of the major world religions were People of Color, white-washed icons and stained glass notwithstanding.

It is important that this be realized because it is essential to the formulation of an identity politics of the spirit. The archetype of the Leatherman has the potential to become a foundation for building purpose and self-worth for Kinky Gay men. Our writers, photographers and artists play an important role in developing the archetype, and I believe that it is no coincidence that they are under attack by the conservative forces that serve spiritual fascism. It was no coincidence that the story tellers, the shamans, and the keepers of the arts of native peoples have always been sought out and destroyed first by the conquerors. We have been *discovered* by the mainstream, but I hope we do not allow history to repeat itself in our community. The seminal potential of the archetype can only develop if combined with the outer world through recognition, story-telling, the visual arts, inclusion in pop culture and through the feedback loop of dreams, fantasies, and the subconscious. In that loop, the archetype is delineated by the contributions of the community, which in turn delineate the parameters of the community, in a process resembling more than anything else Escher's image of a hand with a pen drawing a hand with a pen. It also resembles the

Ouroboros, the serpent swallowing its own tail, forever making and unmaking itself.

On a personal level it is becoming more fully the aspect of the archetype that you embody. For some time now, the mythology and the folklore of Kinky Gay men has told the tale of questing for a fantasy man with admirable qualities and finding at the end of the quest that the seeker has become the fantasy. Herein the Leatherman archetype is echoed in several ways. The hunter becomes the hunted, desire reaches its culmination and dies to be reborn again, and the Leatherman greets the next seeker, bloody rose in hand. Or, he may also await inspiration for his next deep fantasy, his next teacher. The often complex and tumultuous interplay between desires and drives to be top/bottom, daddy/son, master/slave, switch, mutual combatants, comrades in intensity, and the dizzying array of possibilities and probabilities reflect myth and archetype as much as they do personality and cultural context. Our fantasies and our dreams are partly our own and partly the common property of the identity groups to which we belong.

Self-knowledge is considered the crux for personal growth, but is it possible without the inclusion of those parts that are larger than ourselves? I don't think so. I believe that until the spiritual, and in particular the archetypes, are honored and incorporated into the life of the individual and the community, any attempts at understanding through ideologies, philosophies, and psychologies are doomed to failure. We will be replaying the story of the seven academicians caught by a sand storm while trekking through the desert. The seven hold onto each other, eyes clenched shut against the sand, until they run into something that they hope will be refuge from the storm. They find that it is refuge, but their descriptions of it are wildly different. One says that it is like a broad wall, another says that it is like a tree trunk, another says that it is like a stout vine, the others give equally unlikely reports. When the storm dissipates they find that a kindly elephant has given them shelter, a being too large to be grasped by the reach of their hands.

The archetypes also clarify the linkages between individuals and communities. The parts of the elephant only make sense when the whole is grasped. The archetype of the Leatherman for Gay men is a part of a collection of archetypes and mythic stories that describe the sacred truths of being Kinky. An understanding of the family of images and myths that spring from the various subsets of the Kink community could possibly result in a more practical understanding of the parts and the whole of our community. Paradoxically, this understanding helps to ground a community. We need to rediscover, to reclaim or to create our pantheons, our cycles of stories, our lore. If we do undertake this task, more mythic force will become evident in our erotica, our art, and in the jargon and folkways of the Kink community. With that infusion of magic, of the spiritual, into the daily life of the community, the vitality of life as a Kinky person will increase. There are other benefits as well. Experiencing the archetypes can be a powerful revelation spanning differences of gender, orientation, race and culture. I have seen it. I am not suggesting that the ritual I attended many years ago is the only way to bridge this gap; it is merely one. I am suggesting that the archetypes are a common language, an answer to the Babel of our age, and essential to true dialogue.

Stone, Paper, Scissors
Backpatch Club,
SM Organization, GDI

In the Les-Bi-Gay community, the Kink community has organized itself through three basic vehicles: the Backpatch clubs, the SM organizations, and the GDIs.[2] There are others, but I believe these are the three primary colors, and that many other forms of belonging to the organized Kink community are derivative blendings of these three. I also believe that the non-Queer Kink community is adopting these models as well. When I say organized community, I mean not only those people who are members of organizations, but also those people who participate in the activities of the organized community. Beyond outward manifestations of belonging to the organized community, there is an internal shift in perspective that persists whether or not active participation continues. It's like taking the same route home every day, then one day you notice a road you had overlooked a hundred times, and you decide to see where it may take you. Even if you never take it again you know it exists, and your sense of the relationships between places and landmarks is forever changed.

My first encounters with leathermen and leathersex came through pickups at bars, mostly vanilla gay bars. I would look for subtle clues such as a black leather belt or a poise and an attitude indicative of something other than vanilla. In those early explorations, I was looking for rough sex and didn't think of myself as kinky. I began to wear a leather vest, a cowboy hat or

---

2/ GDI stands for "God Damn Independent" and I believe it was coined among the Backpatch clubs.

some other signal/fetish and began to attract the attention of the handful of leathermen who cropped up in the places I was frequenting. As my coming into leather progressed, I began to go to leather bars and met many people who became friends and sexual partners, and for a few years this was enough. During those years, I claimed my identity as a Kinky person and became a part of the community. I acquired the language, norms, and the spirit of the community.

I also paid little attention to club colors on vests or flyers on the bulletin boards announcing runs, conferences, demos and other events. I rarely was present at bar nights or similar events hosted by SM/Leather/Fetish groups because I was not in the habit of going to the leather bars on off nights or early in the evening before the crowds arrived. Though I knew of the existence of an organized Kink community, I had no interest in pursuing connection with it. Like the strange juxtapositions of animals that you'll see at a watering hole in a desert, I socialized alongside others who'd come to relieve their thirst for companionship, obeying the rules of the watering hole truce. There came a day when I took an interest, took an unexplored road, and discovered that I enjoyed the organized life of the community. I became a part of the organized SM/Leather/Kink community, and though my participation has varied in style and intensity over the years, my sense of the community has permanently altered.

Before proceeding with a discussion of the interplay between these three modes, let's look at some of their characteristics. I am not attempting an exploration of the history and the development of the Backpatch clubs, SM organizations, and the GDI's, though it is my hope that scholars in our community will undertake the task soon. The descriptions I'm offering are, of course, skewed by my personal experience and focused for the discussion at hand, but I believe that the essence is accurate. My belief, or bias if you will, is that each of these three modes of participation is needed for the healthy development of the Kink community, and that friction between these three is one of the largest obstacles to progress. Please read with an eye for the underlying or the over-arching patterns only; exceptions can always be found and in real life most groups are a composite of these three types.

Backpatch Clubs

As the name implies, most of these organizations have club colors, in effect a coat of arms. The colors are usually worn on leather vests, and often the club will have established a uniform or a set of guidelines for *formal* wear. Although there are similarities in appearance and in organizational structure to motorcycle clubs, only a small percentage of these clubs ride, let alone require bikes for membership. Many of the conventions of the clubs have their roots in the military, fraternities, lodges, gangs, clerical rites, covens and other groups that have rituals for bonding to create a sense of tribe. The membership of Backpatch clubs tends to be limited, and is generally only granted after a pledge period and with the sponsorship of existing members. High levels of participation are expected. One of the foundations of a Backpatch club's existence is that it is exclusive and selective. Under normal circumstances a person may only be a full member of one Backpatch club at a time. The clubs, though they may affiliate with other groups or create networks, are autonomous. Most Backpatch clubs have a broad range of diversity in the continuum between vanilla and heavy Kink, but relatively less diversity in terms of gender, race and ethnicity.

There are many reasons why people are drawn to Backpatch clubs, but the strongest is probably the promise of fellowship. After the isolation of being in the closet and often the loss of connection to friends or family associated with claiming identity as a sexual minority, the finding of a small group to fill in the social and emotional gap is essential. For some, membership in a Backpatch club is also the first opportunity to *feel like one of the guys.* Membership also provides entry into a more coherent and cohesive social environment than the bar scene, and promises greater opportunities to actually connect with possible friends and lovers.

Backpatch clubs have the potential to meet many of the emotional and spiritual needs of their members. They are among the most tightly knit of non-lover relationships in the sexual minority community, and at their best act as an extended family. The formalized recognition of other Backpatch clubs as *relatives* or as *neighbors* establishes norms and customs that emphasize hospitality and accountability.

Like families, and other small intimate groups, Backpatch clubs are prone to dysfunctions and melodramatic extremes. The flaws and the emotional baggage of the members can reach highly toxic levels in the close confines of the club. The vision of the club's purpose and reason for existence often become personalized and very intense. For some members, self-worth and honor become closely associated with the club. Since not everyone holds the same vision, often not even a similar vision, there is the potential for conflict that can feel, within the closeness of a club, like betrayal or disloyalty. Generally the focus of most Backpatch clubs is apolitical so leatherphobia, homophobia and the whole family of isms are not addressed directly.

SM Organizations

Although I am using the words *SM organization*, I intend it to mean a wide range of Kink focused organizations. SM organizations are often organized along the lines of community organizations with a Board of Directors elected by the membership. The size of the organization can be large, often with a significant number of inactive members. Becoming a member is relatively easy with few requirements other than the payment of dues and agreement to follow the organization's bylaws and policies. People are often full members of more than one organization, and organizational monogamy is not seen as a virtue. Generally, this type of organization has specific educational, political or social goals that are well articulated and arrived at through some open process. The membership of these organizations tends to be more diverse in terms of gender, race, etc., but more narrow in the continuum between vanilla and heavy Kink. The given name or purpose of the organization determines which flavors of Kink will be encouraged or excluded.

SM organizations tend to offer unique opportunities for learning sexual technique and theory from experts in a less threatening, controlled environment. Demonstrations, workshops, and discussion groups are the main part of most SM organizations' schedules. For people seeking an activist focus for their Kink identity there are few better vehicles than membership in an SM organization. Political action and networking with non-Kink organizations are widespread among SM organizations. A part of the mission of many SM organizations is the improvement of the status of Kinky people through cultural and legislative change. For people who are not seeking to have a good portion of their primary social needs met through their membership in a group, SM organizations are more comfortable than Backpatch clubs. Normally, the expectations are that members will participate only in those activities they personally find interesting.

Because of size and organizational structure, SM groups can muster money, energy and talent for various projects with relative ease. They have the greatest potential to push an agenda of political and cultural change for the liberation of Kinky people. Being a community organization rather than a *tribe* places the strength and determination of the organization in its ideals and goals rather than in the individuals and their interrelations. The tendency to put an emphasis on skill and accomplishment rather than looks or popularity in SM organizations makes it possible for people to shine who would otherwise be locked out in other settings.

There are always trade-offs, gains and losses, that come with the nature of any group's pattern. In my estimation the largest failing of SM organizations comes from the fact that they are modeled after the corporate structures that allow individuals who are crafty to outmaneuver the decision making process. I know. I've done it myself, much to my subsequent embarrassment. The less personal nature of large membership organizations also accommodates a considerable amount of alienation and tolerates high levels of apathy. Interactions between SM organizations and other groups often lack the personal touch.

GDIs

It may seem unusual to include the category of unaffiliated individuals in a discussion of ways of belonging to the organized Kink community, but GDIs meet the one important test: they *see* the organized community. They have learned and to some degree contribute to the culture of the organized community. Many GDIs are former members of Backpatch clubs or SM organizations. Indeed, some GDIs are minimally members of SM organizations, but are unaffiliated in the sense that they have no deep sense of connection to any organization's agenda. There are also GDIs who have not been members of any group but regularly attend events, read newsletters and periodicals that cover the organized Kink community, and have acquired the language and folkways of the community. There are probably more GDIs than there are active members of the Backpatch Clubs and the SM organizations put together. There is a loose sense of camaraderie with other GDIs, and a certain pride in being independent.

Not everyone enjoys or is temperamentally suited to the tight-knit nature of a Backpatch club or the ideology of an SM organization. Many people also find that the requirements of time, money or participation cannot be brought into balance with their other commitments. Being able to support organized activities by attendance, subscriptions, and so on benefits both the GDI and the organizations.The person who is a GDI often has the best of both worlds.

Having access to the cultural milieu of the organized community but with fewer entanglements, allegiances and emotional investment, GDIs can more easily gain perspectives on issues and situations in the Kink community. The neutral status of most GDIs allows them passage into and through many territories. GDIs are also selected at times as compromise candidates, appointees, and contest winners to avoid internecine conflict, serving their community through their nonalignment. A GDI can also assume a trickster role with greater general acceptance, and defuse tensions or point out foibles through humor.

A lack of affiliation does not necessarily mean a lack of attitude, or a definite slant. Some GDIs offer harsh criticism of the work of organizations without a sense of or an acknowledgement of the hard work with limited resources that goes into producing events, activities, and publications. Sometimes there is an "I'm here to be entertained—not participate" attitude that is subtly corrosive of the energy and the *vibes* of an event or gathering. Having an investment in the outcome helps to temper the actions of people who are members of groups. Some GDIs have a lesser sense of belonging to or investment in the community because membership based on a nebulous concept of Kink community is considerably less grounding and balancing than membership in the concrete form of a group. So, depending upon their character, they may be prone to thoughtless behavior.

At a horrific community meeting I attended several years ago, a meeting so acrimonious there should have been a psychic smog alert and so filled with intrigue that it should have been raided by the karma police, I retreated inward and sought refuge in humor. In my mind's eye I saw a group of people playing *stone, paper, scissors.* For those whose childhood didn't include this game, here's a quick summary. Two people face each other and at the count of three, they hold out a hand held either in a fist like a stone, or flat like paper, or with two fingers extended like scissors. Who wins is determined by the combination of hands: stone breaks scissors, paper wraps stone, scissors cut paper, with a stalemate if the hands are the same. What I was witnessing at the meeting very much resembled this game. The Backpatch clubs I envisioned as stone, the SM organizations as paper, and the GDI's as scissors. You may draw a long chain of associations from this metaphor. The solidarity a Backpatch club can summon when it perceives itself to be threatened can be as solid as a rock. The reams of rationales, mailings and ploys that an SM organization can generate to cover all the bases is wrapping paper craft at its best. The GDI, lacking the burden of the stone or the house of cards of an organization, is free to cut a figure through the paper like scissors. The scissors will lose their edge if the GDI tries to cut the stone, and the Backpatch club will crush scissors that have cut too far. The stalemate or lose/lose situation that arises when club faces club, organization faces organization, or GDI faces GDI is equally clear. Each way of belonging to the organized Kink community has its strengths and its weaknesses. As a game, stone, paper, scissors may prove a harmless diversion. As a way of negotiating differences and agendas it is at least frustrating, if not infuriating.

The conflicts and misunderstandings between the Backpatch clubs, SM organizations and GDIs fritter away much-needed time and energy. There are people of good will who work to span the differences among all the communities, but they are in the minority. The meeting that triggered this flight of ideas did not produce any useful results. The criticisms that these three camps level at each other are understandable, even sensible, from their respective viewpoints, but they are still counter-productive. The deadlocks that have resulted from these games of *stone, paper, scissors* have contributed to greater and greater separations among the three camps. It's not exactly a cold war, perhaps more like detente, but in this time of increased targeting of Kinky people by Right wing forces don't we need to band together? The *organized* Kink community is a small percentage of the SM/Leather/Fetish community; we don't need to break into even smaller numbers. I recall my naive amazement when I discovered that not even the networking organizations communicated or cooperated with each other in a significant way. Backpatch clubs talk to Backpatch clubs and SM organizations talk to SM organizations.

Why does this state of affairs exist? In part it may relate to a common human failing. We tend to be most critical of those who are almost like us or those who are family. The greater the differences in characteristics and qualities between groups or between individuals, the less the expectation or desire there is for that group or individual to conform to your standards. Whether it's the war in Ireland, the ideological blood baths between Left wing groups, or the heated theological debates of different flavors of the same faith, it's all about the *little difference* and the *one true way*. When someone who is similar in significant ways makes different choices or holds different beliefs it is a challenge, the road not taken. It evokes a desire to defend the choices you've made and to convert others to your way. In the Kink community this human failing is reinforced by leatherphobia resulting in Kink-on-Kink conflict in all the forms that horizontal hostility takes. Internalized leatherphobia, along with a few other isms and phobias, magnifies this problem in a number of ways. One of the classic effects of isms and phobias is the inclination to stereotype, to view members of a group as a monolithic whole. In this case that means viewing other Kinky people as more similar than they really are, denying their diversity and increasing the desire to enforce standards of conformity.

91

When a member of a Backpatch club makes a disparaging statement about an SM organization's lack of camaraderie or a member of an SM organization snipes that a certain Backpatch club is just leather dress-up with no real kink, this dynamic is illustrated well. The standards of one are unfairly imposed upon the other. When a GDI complains that a Backpatch club is just a clique for people who can't make it on their own, they are on as solid a turf as the SM organization member that has a GDI banned or shunned because they spread disruptive ideas. Backpatch clubs are nothing but bar flys and ego games. SM organizations are nothing but political game playing disguised behind a cloud of high sounding words. GDIs are free loaders that just want to be entertained without doing any of the work. The hurtful, destructive comments that often abound at meetings, events, at the bar and virtually anywhere we gather serve our enemies well. It should be no surprise that some people find a discussion group a terrible bore and that others find a Backpatch club officers' installation banquet a mind-numbing hell. One of the broadly held truths in the Kink community is that one person's turn on is another's turn off. We recognize the existence of a wide range of sexual and affectional tastes; should we not recognize the diversity of tastes and opinions in how to organize our community?

Recognition of this diversity is becoming more important because the entire community, and the organized community in particular, is undergoing rapid, dramatic changes in its composition. The number of new clubs and organizations that are hybrids that do not fit in the old molds is growing. Groups like the various Bear clubs and organizations that are definitely fetish interest groups but highly variable in their SM/leather focus are an example of a new development that may or may not find welcome in the existing network. Some of the Bear groups are leaning towards the Backpatch mode, and others toward organizational models more common in the vanilla Queer community. Groups are forming and flourishing that combine

elements of the SM organizations and the Backpatch clubs:
groups for Kinky people of the same faith, groups for Kinky
people in recovery, groups with a tight social knit but a purpose
beyond the confines of the club. There are even groups designed
with the GDI in mind which have minimal requirements and
maximized networking. There are virtual organizations in the
form of computer bulletin boards and cyberspace which foster
intellectual and emotional exchanges having as real an impact on
the participants as an in-the-flesh gathering. There are more
women and more People of Color taking an active role in the
organized Kink community, and with this influx comes new
ideas. The wider debate of questions of sexuality spurred by the
increased visibility of Bisexuals and Transgendered people is
transforming the Kink community's understanding of its
Pansexual composition. With new blood and new energy come
fresh perspectives from unexplored vantage points, additional
goals, and pioneering methods better fitted to addressing a
broader agenda.

Or, if the old intolerance and territoriality continues we'll
have greater division and a more fractious social climate. My
worry is that we are still playing *stone, paper, scissors* while the
world about us is getting more complicated, more intricate and
more dangerous. How will we play the game when three hands,
four hands, more hands, are held out? What will we say when
a player holds out both hands? How will we arbitrate when in
addition to stone, paper, and scissors, we also have hammer,
stapler, fax machine and magic wand to consider? Perhaps we
should leave the game-playing for our bedrooms and dungeons.
Perhaps we should re-evaluate what we are trying to accomplish
through our organizations, and see if our actions match our
words. The old ways of organizing have no special sway over
the whirlpool of change spinning through the community any
more than the Old Guard can control leather fashion or mores by
decree. Thank goodness.

Although challenging in the extreme, this explosion of

change is probably a sign of health, an indication that we've hit cultural critical mass. Many of the factors that shaped organizational structures in the past were based on scarcity of human resources and isolationism as a defense against the antagonism of the mainstream culture. In the last decade so many people have come out into Kink that a wide variety of specialized organizations are viable. As people win power back from the internalized oppressions of the mainstream culture they use that power to seek or to become what they genuinely desire. In the case of the Kink community this means more and more flavors of kink as people allow the "loves that dare not speak their names" to not only speak, but to write poetry, to edit newsletters, even to skywrite.

The access to ideas and people afforded by greater numbers of out people, more Kink focused media, and public events is creating an SM/Leather/Fetish global village. In this climate the old-style coordinating councils, federations, and networking groups for Kink organizations seem out of step with the possibilities and more importantly, the new imperatives. Indeed, an intrepid individual with a computer, a modem and a few periodicals can take the information pulse of the community as easily as an organization. The individual, however, does not have the potential for collective action that an organization has, nor the capacity to synthesize a group vision. The task at hand then for existing organizations is to rework and retool to remain viable or go the way of the dinosaur. The task for all organizations is to recognize that communities are like ecologies. Each type of organization and individual mode of participation is important, and the vitality of the community is to a good part measured by diversity and symbiosis.

How do we begin to encourage healthy interactions among the various organizations, camps and tribes? One route is to remember that organizations exist to promote a common good that in turn benefits individual members. Possibly what is needed is an explicit statement that the common good of the

SM/Leather/Fetish community depends on solidarity and respect for the power of our differences. Old habits die hard, and we must use every technique we can muster to bear in mind a commitment to cooperation. However fashionable outlaw imagery and mystique may be in some quarters, I would offer that we are warriors, not bandits. Perhaps some groups will develop a code of ethics or conduct that explicitly includes commitment to process and cooperation. Amending the often dreary oaths taken by club officers to acknowledge responsibility to the Kink community could revitalize those ceremonies. There are a thousand and one subtle changes in attitudes, norms and behaviors that would eventually be brought about by shining a little light on this piece of the common good. And it will have to be a thousand and one ways that the wheel is reinvented because it must be a wheel that suits the myriad paths that we are traveling. However beneficial that may be, I believe that the greatest gains will come through respecting the power of our differences. In so doing we help to create an atmosphere of positive regard that weakens leatherphobia. In acknowledging the differences we reduce the fear and the mistrust of the unknown, and the false knowing of the stereotype. With luck, in time we'll trust each other enough to show each other the unique power that arises from our difference, perhaps even to share it.

Kink Nation:
Identity Politics In Flatland

Over one hundred years ago, Edwin A. Abbott wrote a short novel entitled: *Flatland—A Romance Of Many Dimensions* that would be mandatory reading if I were the education czar. It is filled with images, ingenuity and insights that are capable of coaxing new ideas out of old ones. Without ruining the story for those who haven't read *Flatland*, I'd like to share some of its metaphors that may shed light on the chaos and confusion afflicting the SM/Leather/Fetish community. Flatland is a two dimensional reality; length and width exist but height does not. We can imagine the citizens of this imaginary land as triangles, ovals, squares and other simple geometric figures moving in the endless flat plane of their world. Imagine that one day a visitor, an explorer from a three dimensional reality, visits Flatland. This visitor, a Sphere, attempts a dialogue with a very staid Square. Of course, the Square looks at the Sphere and sees a circle, which makes the Sphere's story of being from another reality a little hard to believe. Since the Sphere does have a genuine desire to communicate with the Square, it moves up and down through the third dimension to prove itself. Much to the Square's amazement and shock the Circle changes size. The apparent Circle shrinks to a Point, becoming one-dimensional, then expands to form a Circle once more. The Square is convinced that something strange is happening, but the idea of three dimensions, or the concept of a Sphere, is still beyond its comprehension.

It is my belief that we are simultaneously both Squares and Spheres as we interact with each other within the narrow plane of concepts we currently call identity, community and politics. Please bear with me in making these initial comparisons, but I think you'll find that a flight of fancy is needed to gain enough

Beneath The Skins

distance for a fresh perspective. However oppressive the present social and political climate may feel for Kinky people, it has improved sufficiently in the last several decades to create such an explosion in possible identities and social contexts that we have expanded beyond the flat plane. The old paradigms are no longer adequate. Worst of all, the philosophies, the ideologies and their proponents that were the most progressive in the previous phase of development don't know that they are outdated yet. As individuals, we have an intuitive understanding that we are more than labels or flat representations, but it is rare to have a cognitive understanding of our whole selves. This lack of awareness shapes how we see the outside world. We are like Spheres seeing through the eyes of Squares. When we approach others on the common ground of being Kinky, it is usually not a three-dimensional landscape peopled with three-dimensional beings, but a flat world with flat characters whose constitution and appearance are determined by our perspective, and not their reality.

We construct ourselves out of the many identities and labels that comprise our sphere of self. Additionally, we often move into roles with their associated set of behaviors and interactions when we engage in significant political or social encounters. Because we, as a community, have not as of yet constructed a *sphere* to integrate Kink identity into a sense of self in a global way, there is a propensity to try to dress up our other identities and roles in leather as a makeshift measure. Although this stopgap may be useful for individuals it hinders the Kink community because it is a composite community. Like a song, a composite community is made up of many distinct and important elements, each note and each word gaining beauty and meaning from context, interval and chord. The notes and the words are neither lessened by their association in the song nor do they lose their intrinsic qualities, they only gain richness. However, the Kink community's song either hasn't been written yet, or is only known by a few, or perhaps is drowned out in the din of conflict. When we come together, it is rarely like musicians striving for the harmonious beauty of collective expression; more often than not, it resembles a bad day at the United Nations or a Tower of Babel reenactment society. When we come together for important matters in the Kink community wearing the badges of our other identities *first*, turf and agenda wars ensue. When we insist on speaking in specialized languages, filled with the jargon of our respective ideologies, and expect others to do the same, or insist on interpreting their languages using a different grammar and vocabulary, then misfortune is sure to follow.

I can think of my self, in alphabetical order, as a Bear, Bottom, Cuban, Environmentalist, Feminist, Gay, Kinky, Leftist, Male, Progressive, Rural, Sex Radical, Top, Vegetarian, Wiccan, among other things. The combined diversity and personal complexity at an inclusive gathering of the Kink community can be staggering if viewed as a tumble of labels and banners for different camps. The tangle of circles of identity in this Flatland becomes even harder to understand as we move through different issues. Each issue is a different plane, so the *shape* that individuals take will be different, further obscuring the connecting themes and inter-relationships. It can be confusing for the individuals as well, as they switch hats and roles trying to keep up with debates that pivot on a word. The culprit for this frustrating state of affairs is pluralism. The failure of pluralism as a guideline for the life of composite communities, such as the SM/Leather/Fetish community, has contributed to the conceptual bankruptcy that has confined us to Flatland. While pluralism sounds like a great step forward, it is actually a dead end. There are two basic tenets underlying pluralism: strong belief in cultural relativity and in the autonomy of cultural groups brought about through compartmentalization. I am using culture in the broadest sense, meaning a coherent cluster of language, beliefs, folkways, sensibilities or other parameters that offer distinct possibilities for roles and identities. Cultural relativism states that all cultures have their own behaviors, beliefs and values that cannot and should not be judged by other cultures. Cultural compartmentalization creates the image of an endless series of cubicles, each containing a culture separate from the others.

Both relativism and compartmentalization appeal to sexual minorities because they put forth a rationale promoting safe space and tolerance. This form of pluralism has almost become sacrosanct in the liberal and progressive wings of industrialized nations, various liberation movements, and academia. It is also sterile, promotes a studied form of apathy, and is ultimately a cowardly form of denial. Real dialogue requires the risk involved with making judgments, discernments, and comparisons between groups across cultural divides. It means dealing with the differences, not ignoring them, deciding that they are immaterial, or declaring them untranslatable. Real cultural exchange cannot occur if the histories, the developmental lines of ideas or forces, and the current matrix of inter-relations are arbitrarily severed so that each culture can be squeezed into its own insular little box.

For the Kink community this type of pluralism has been expressed through contrived attempts at gender parity, racial and ethnic quotas, sexual orientation diversity and geographical representation. This arrangement has also resulted in correspondingly segregated statements of politics and ethics by representative bodies of the Kink community that have invisible but undeniable lines running between the sections that each interest group fought for. Make no mistake that it is an improvement over the homogeneous, mostly White urban male pattern of not too long ago, but there is no synthesis of the various flavors and strands. When we engage in this type of coming together, we are not a tribe or a composite community, we are an artificial structure with about as much cohesion as the Democratic party during presidential primaries. To become more than that we have to take chances, become intimate at the level of sharing the chromosomes of culture, our values, ideals, fears and hopes. We have to be willing to collaborate, not just to coexist. If we do not, we will not create a living whole that gives sense and meaning to the Kink body politic. Instead, we will piece together a Frankenstein.

In many ways the SM/Leather/Fetish community is following in the developmental footsteps of the Queer community. This may be a result of the high percentage of organizers and activists in the Kink community who are Les-Bi-Gay and the probability that sexual minorities will have similar experiences in this society. One social phenomena that has swept the Les-Bi-Gay community which may also reach the Kink community is the emergence of rage as a motivating force in organizations and activities. The wellsprings of emotion that have erupted as geysers of rage in the Queer community have been activated by the genocidal response to HIV exhibited by most of the powers that be, and a steady stream of political losses generated by a well-funded and coordinated Religious Right. Existing community organizations were unable or unwilling to channel this wild energy, so many direct action groups such as ACT-Up and Queer Nation were born. Naked raw force is something that we cannot abide—we clothe it in movements, organizations, and names as soon as we are able. It's a human thing.

As Kinky people develop increasing cohesion and self-awareness of themselves as a cultural unit there will be an explosion in the number of movement or politically-focused organizations. For every action there is a reaction, so there will also be a dramatic increase in Right-wing attacks on the Kink community. I did not say equal reaction, because unlike the Kink organizations that will be in their infancy, the Conservative organizations are well-established and boast a committed membership. It is safe to assume that though there will be a few victories there will be even more defeats, at least initially. Increasing identity and sense of self as a Kinky person will also mean that the defeats and attacks will be felt more keenly. Ultimately there will be a reservoir of rage and also of deep disbelief that the Kink organizations can be effective in dealing with the community problems or insuring community safety. Given that the model already exists and that there is an open border between the Kink and the Queer communities, it is almost a foregone conclusion that there will be something like a Kink Nation. The recognition by direct action groups that we are a nation, a people, could be a powerful positive step. But this recognition is shaped and colored by the perception of our enemies because it is a reaction to their rage and their stereotypical view of Kinky people.

Many people have already formed opinions on the merits or the shortcomings of direct action groups. Insomuch as I am able, I am trying to reserve judgment on whether these groups will result in a net loss or net gain. It is my bias to believe that different approaches working on different fronts lead to the most social and political change. Unfortunately, rage, like fire, must be respected and shaped lest it leave the hearth or the forge and become a destroyer rather than an ally. At this time most of the direct action groups in the Queer community are as likely to burn Les-Bi-Gay people and groups as they are our traditional opponents. Anger is a powerful force that can be harnessed for positive or negative ends. Rage tends to bring human consciousness into one red-hot point of awareness. Without the anchor of an understanding that rage is part of something greater, the three-dimensional construct of community or nation collapses into Flatland. Instead of meaningful interaction, the groups and the players are reduced to two-dimensional characters whose scope of dialogue is limited to the one plane held in common, mutual deprecation.

If confrontational direct-action groups do become a strong force in the Kink community, they will face some unique obstacles. Many SM/Leather/Fetish people walk a tightrope in balancing the exchange of power in their sexual lives with their public lives. The rush of exercising political power in direct action can be akin to that of a scene or SM play. Being the butch, bad ass, outlaw means different things depending upon context and intent. For Kink Nation-type groups the potential for encouraging the blurring of the lines between the personal and the political is a great risk for both the individual and the community. The rule of *never playing in anger* takes on added meanings. The competitiveness of trying to out *bottom* or out *top* others in enduring or inflicting more in the context of direct action or political work, theoretically for the sake of the Kink liberation movement, could produce unhealthy results. The outlaw/renegade aspect of the equation could lead to a *kinkier than thou* and *are you with us or against us mentality* that is often coupled with an intolerance of those who choose to work for the community in different ways. Say what you will, but it has been my experience that the human psyche is a whole, so ideas and actions do not stay confined to one arena but mix and mingle throughout the person's behavior and attitudes. The shadow of the community, all the orphaned and repressed feelings, becomes the power behind the throne unless dealt with directly. The fire of rage unless mastered by a desire to heal and to purify can become a wildfire that destroys indiscriminately.

So how do we proceed past the limits of Flatland? I think that the community has already had the answer on its lips. Kinky people are a tribe, or more accurately many tribes that form a nation. Some may argue that the concept of tribes and tribalism is archaic or primitive and unsuited to modern life. I suggest that it is a *high touch*, flexible and sophisticated way of looking at commonalities. There are many models of tribal life and ethics that can accommodate great diversity while providing a framework to weave the strands into a meaningful pattern. Some call it the expropriation of cultural property and take offense that any dare call themselves a tribe or adopt folkways or rites associated with tribal cultures who are not currently tribal people. I would agree that shallow or disrespectful play acting with a sacred resource is distasteful, but the essence of *tribe* belongs to all humanity. First, everyone on Earth is descended

103

of tribal ancestors however many generations removed, and in the Americas most of us are of mixed race and/or ethnicity. Secondly, ideas and culture, unlike material goods, are not destroyed or diminished when imitated or copied—they are destroyed by lack of use, lack of appreciation or outright campaigns of eradication. Third, all tribes and all cultures in existence for the last several millennia are hybrids and they all had a beginning even if we can't follow the trail back to the exact when and where. Perhaps now is the time for new tribes to come into being. Human cultural progress and creativity are due in good part to the cross-pollination of ideas, ideas that like pollen do not honor political or cultural borders. Being a tribe is a question of spirit, not political analysis or anthropology, so I do not believe that the materialism implicit in calling it expropriation will hold up over time.

The spirit of being a tribe gives us a third dimension, the fullness that the Sphere tried to communicate to the Square in Flatland. Sadly, spirit or essence cannot be communicated in the linear form of words. The description "tribe" may be used by many for many years before it is more than a buzzword. Like family, the concept of tribe is only grasped by living it. Those who have the experience of feeling their destinies and the roots of their being interwoven with others in the Kink community will know what tribe means. They can through their actions create opportunities for others to discover their membership in the tribes of the Kink Nation—a Nation built not on the red-hot point of rage or the precipice of anger but on the solid back of the ground. Kinky people are risk-takers, and perhaps through new ways of relating, meta-tribes will result from synthesizing so much diversity through the lenses of sexualities. If so, a new gift will have been brought to the common cultural heritage of humankind.

National Groups: Why We Need Them

I believe that the SM/Leather/Fetish community has come as far as it can in its development without the existence of well-supported national organizations. I am not suggesting that we are at a standstill. There are still many geographical areas where the community will become more active and more visible. The businesses and publications that cater to the Kink community have not reached a plateau yet. In fact, as is true for every viable community, there are individuals, groups and projects at every stage of development from infancy to old age simultaneously. But I believe we are headed for a glass ceiling. Further progress depends upon bolstering existing groups with a national focus, and the creation of new national groups which view themselves specifically as *movement* organizations. A shift in perception is needed in order to see what is missing, because building a movement is not the same as networking, putting on conferences, or having play parties, although each of those activities can play an important role. It is not my intent to comment on current groups or upon proposals for future groups or to give an opinion on their relative merits. It is my intent to focus attention on serious gaps in the weave of the Kink community's organizational structure with the hope that they will eventually be mended.

Although there is much that can be accomplished by local and regional groups, the very nature of such groups prevents them from taking on projects of national scale and scope. The SM organizations, the MCs, the LCs, discussion groups, and other Kink-focused organizations generally have a hard enough time organizing and implementing existing activities. Calendars tend to be crowded with events and business meetings scheduled carefully around busy lives and inter-organizational etiquette and turf. There is only so much room on the plate or on the agenda, and though you can go back for more it will be seconds. If they are to be faithful to their own purposes, local and regional groups tend to address national concerns only after having met local or regional obligations. Even if normal priorities are suspended, it is unlikely that non-national groups will have the wherewithal to properly address a national task. Most local or regional groups do not have sufficient access to information to reach informed decisions about a wide range of topics. The resources to carry out complicated, long-term projects are usually lacking and the consistency of effort that would be provided by staff is unheard of. Although volunteerism is the backbone of many movements, the muscle is in the paid staff.

I have heard it argued that we don't really need national groups per se, just better coordination and networking between groups. This has been somewhat successful for special events such as marches and celebrations, and less successful in combating specific incidents of censorship or legal outrage. Quasi-national groups such as networks, coordinating councils, special committees, etc. are not suited to long-term tasks like developing vision or consensus. Much of the energy available for this type of group is siphoned off by the strenuous effort needed to recruit participation, and then to encourage cooperation among those that do answer the call. Cutting corners on the effort to generate broad participation leads to active or passive resistance from those who were intentionally or unintentionally excluded, which often diminishes the effectiveness of the group. Once you have gathered together all interested parties, then despite high ideals, there is the inevitable jockeying for position and for the protection of turf and of prerogatives. The question of ownership and control always arises in composite groups. The organizations that provide the most money or energy either expect to have more say or are perceived as wanting more than a fair amount of input on decisions. Composite groups also tend to have problems accommodating and reconciling the participation of individual community activists with that of organizations. The fatal flaw in networks, consortiums and other composite groups, from the point of view of movement building, is that they have no sense of themselves or of self-preservation. Just as individuals must take care of themselves first in order to be helpful to others, organizations must do the same if they are to do lasting good. To function with integrity and strength, national groups must be autonomous.

It is unlikely that existing non-SM/Leather/Fetish-identified national organizations will be willing or able to address satisfactorily the needs of the Kink community. They too have overly full plates with limited resources, and we are not at the top of the to-do list. I do believe that it is essential that we strive for inclusion, participation, and presence in the workings of national organizations, especially Queer or progressive groups. I don't believe that it is reasonable to expect much more than that, though on occasion there will be issues or incidents with ramifications that span multiple communities. At those times there can be significant help from these national organizations. Like organizations and individuals in identity groups such as People of Color, Women, Les-Bi-Gay, Transgendered, etc., we must approach the progress of our community through inclusion and through building our own national organizations. Even if a non-Kink national group were willing to strongly commit to our issues, we would be ill served because our issues would be defined by those outside the community, a risky business indeed.

Defining our own issues, creating our own manifestos and our own mission statements, are necessary for our progress as a community. Leather/SM/Fetish people, as a sexual minority, have been following a course similar to that of the Queer community. In the last fifty years or so we have gone from being isolated individuals carefully seeking out our counterparts, to a secret and well hidden community, to old guard, new guard, avant garde, and to radical sex politics. I am no historian, but I suspect we've already had our Stonewall, and time will tell us which event or combination of events we'll call our watershed. We are having our holocaust, that I do not doubt. What we have not yet experienced, as far as I can tell, is the birth of our movement, though we have seen a few worthy attempts. What do we as a community want in the long run? What is our vision of Kink utopia? While certainly very important, work on legislative concerns, civil liberties, educating novices, arranging social events and other practical matters do not create a vision of cultural and social change. And in the long run oppressed communities must have vision, hope and spirit to provide guidance, drive and motivation. National groups with a focus on building a movement can serve as catalysts for visioning as well as the more mundane tasks.

For a movement to attain wide-ranging visibility and credibility it must have a national presence with the media, politicians and other large organizations. Visibility and Credibility are gained slowly through persistence and struggle. Happily, this hard work pays off in many ways. As national organizations gain greater status and influence there is a trickle-down impact on all Kink organizations which then share in increased status by association. Over time the relationships among local, regional and national groups develop their own dynamic. National groups have access to the pulse of news and issues and can respond quickly to the national media which often generates local media interest. National groups can spin stories to local contacts, acting as media clearinghouses. Local and regional groups in turn are the front line that can provide the national groups with the hidden details, the background information, and the human touch that can be distilled into powerful statements for press releases. Political progress requires coordinated pressure in Washington, D.C., on the state and local levels, only possible with the focus of a national group. Lobbying on the national level requires meetings with people within the Beltway, but the promise of constituent action at home. Lobbying at the state and local levels is strongly affected by actions in D.C. and in other states. Agencies, organizations, and institutions will often ask local or regional groups if they are affiliated with any national groups to get a sense of their leanings. And more often than not, national groups only take other national groups seriously.

Just as an individual needs a permanent mailing address and identification to exist in the eyes of the law, and more importantly in the eyes of the information highway that modern life depends upon, movements need national organizations to act as the home address and phone number of the community. An enormous amount of information, contacts, opportunities, and useful leads is now being lost for lack of a valid address. Of course, not everyone wants to be found, to have an official existence. Issues of privacy and leatherphobia will require or create a desire for invisibility for many, as is their right. The existence of national beacons, or targets as it may be, will keep the attention on those who are ready and willing to be on the front lines. Although it is my hope that more people will come out as Kinky because that is the single most effective tool for change, those who are in the closet can assist national groups from the safety of their home until they are prepared to do otherwise.

Of all the things that national movement organizations could bring about, a *place at the table* is probably the most important. Whether welcome or not, our existence as a community, a class or a people is not part of the common reality of decision-making bodies. One of the most damaging forms of discrimination or oppression is that of being ignored or shunned. We are not considered when the guest list is made for panels, open hearings, councils, boards and so on. Sometimes we come begging to the table of public discourse. Sometimes we bring our own utensils and seat ourselves. The day when a place has been set for us will come sooner if we have national groups elbowing their way in now. A place at the table is both a concrete and a symbolic act signifying that a community can no longer be ignored. It means that the lie that we are not a community but a scattering of fringe elements can be repeated but no longer believed, even by the liars. Some may say that we already have this recognition, but I do not consider the highly provisional acceptance of Kinky people in Queer settings to be a place at the table. It is progress, and it was gained through confrontation and persistence, but it should not be thought of as having arrived.

In your mind's eye review your list of the community's priorities and needs, not the even longer wish list, and ask yourself if we have the structures in place to address those tasks. Your list will be different from mine, but I'm fairly sure that some of these will be shared:

• The removal of local and national laws that prohibit Kinky acts between consenting adults, or that regard them as assault.

• Recognition of our long term relationships, including relationships of more than two people, in law, in policies and in society.

• The removal of mental health diagnoses that declare healthy Kinky people to have pathological conditions.

• The fostering of scholarship on Kink and a legitimate national archive.

• The repeal of laws that make the possession of erotica and sex toys a crime.

• The inclusion of the Kink community as a distinct and viable part of the diversity that makes up our society.

• An end to the hostility and discrimination against Kinky people in law, in policies and in society.

• The fostering of a Kinky sensibility in our community's art and culture as free from societally enforced distortions as possible.

• A wide variety of supportive routes for people to find their way into our community in their coming out process.

• Our share of the pie regarding our health concerns.

• Healing and education to reduce the racism, sexism, Bi-phobia, and all the other isms and phobias that limits unity in the Kink community. Hopefully, an appreciation for the wonder of all the cultures comprising our community will develop over time.

The national groups at the heart of most movements are almost always woefully underfunded and understaffed. It is not likely that if we bring the national groups we need into existence, they will be any different from the rest in this regard. However, they will not forget what isn't being done, and will endeavor to remind the community of what is needed.

Throughout this discussion, I have referred to national *groups*, always plural, because I believe that at every level from local to national there are different niches requiring different approaches. Though there is a bias to cry "Waste!" and "Duplication!" whenever more than one group is working on an issue, it is quite likely that the groups differ in their techniques. If two groups really are substantially similar, then a merger will seem the rational course for both groups. Perhaps what is really being said is "Control!" and "My plan's better!." This bias leads to a terrible waste of energy spent squabbling. A powerful cultural myth used to oppress us is the myth of the *Plan* which states that there is a single best way to do everything. This one little seed grows into the strangling vine of political, social and spiritual fascism that chokes out all diversity. Although many Kinky people tolerate a wide range of sexual differences, many tendrils of the *Plan* are still tangled around their other perceptions and beliefs. This is not to say that we should not plan, rather that we should have many plans with many options. Cooperation and compromise are hard lessons to learn, especially for a community puffed up with the defenses of being butch, bad outlaws.

We really never know what is coming next. We can extrapolate from trends and make best guesstimates about the future, but something always surprises us when the future becomes the present—so much for the myth of the Plan. The uncertainties of the future contain both opportunities and

111

disasters, and one of the job descriptions for movement organizations is to lean as far forward as they can from the cutting edge of the present and to then scout out the next steps. The creation of five-year strategic plans, handbooks on organizing around specific concerns and the shepherding of new ideas and new activists are among the many activities best handled by national groups. When crisis situations occur there may be only a golden hour, week or month in which to respond. If we waste time creating ad hoc networks or regional responses we lose momentum before we even begin. In these makeshift responses, how likely is it that we'll have experienced spokespeople and competent activists at the fore? Having been to a number of meetings of the Kink community to select representatives and to create committees, I am skeptical, very skeptical. It is a given that there will be conflict over diversity in all its forms, over geographical representation, organizational turf, the decision making process. So far, so bad, but not too unlike comparable movements. It is the criteria for selection often used by the Kink community that worries me the most. The number of sashes, belts and contest titles someone has won should not be considered the credentials for an organizer. Some titleholders do make excellent organizers but they are the exception, and fewer still make the cut as activists. How often someone's picture has peppered the pages of magazines and journals also does not reveal their experience or their exposure to the issues of the day. Even leadership in a SM/Leather/Fetish group does not necessarily prepare a person for the work of a movement since the majority of existing groups focus on social events, demos and runs, with little political work.

A by-product of the formation of movement-focused national groups will be the creation of opportunities for Kinky people to become radicalized politically and to gain much needed skills in activism. Another is that Kinky people who are currently organizers and activists in other movements will finally be able to exercise their talents within the SM/Leather/Fetish community. Given the many talented Kinky people I've met in other political arenas, I suspect that there would be a huge home-coming for these activists if the opportunity arose. Ultimately an enriched environment would develop where there would be sufficient intellectual ferment to infuse the Kink community with innovative ideas. People in the national arena generally return to local and regional groups after a time, sharing information and mentoring, and eventually a self-sustaining cycle of community development would become established. The formation of local and regional groups with a movement or activist focus would also be fostered by the existence of a nationwide movement for Kinky people.

There are a thousand and one heartaches, obstacles and labors associated with the creation of a movement, and the creation of viable national groups is probably the most arduous of all. Will there be failures and wasted money and energy? Yes, in abundance. Will the community be fractious and provincial? We are who we are at this time. Will we see results soon? No, it'll be more like a drop of water on a stone, slowly wearing it away. Is it worth it? That's the chicken and the egg question. Where do we get the vision for a movement to create the national organizations that will carry the torch aloft so that the community can see? Personally, I believe in pulling yourself up by the bootstraps—so long as the boots are winged with grace.

The Well Stocked Discussion Group

Discussion groups have played an important formative role in my life. This is not to say that they were all good experiences. In fact, some of them stunk and stung. Be that as it may, I derived benefit from the focus and intensity they brought to my thoughts and my feelings. A discussion group can be like a lens, correcting distortions, bringing clarity, or concentrating everything into one white-hot point. A discussion group can be like a crucible, melting ores to produce new alloys or purifying, burning off the dross of life events. A discussion group can also be boring and ineffectual, which is a terrible loss. The quality of life for Kinky people depends in great store on their inner life. How far have they come in their healing from the ravages of the closet? What foundations of positive emotion have they laid to support their self worth? To what degree have the various pieces of their lives been reconciled into wholes? Certainly, discussion groups are not the only place that a person can work through the issues of being a SM/Leather/Fetish person in a hostile, sex-negative environment, but they have many virtues. There are few opportunities for stimulating, in-depth conversations in most social gatherings, and business meetings rarely have enough time to complete the tasks on the agenda let alone allow for heartfelt exploration. Although some people do need the professional help of a trained counselor to work through the issues of being a Kinky person, there are many who do not. To imply that a professional is always or often needed would unnecessarily suggest pathology. Coming out is a life-long process of ever-growing self-awareness, a natural process with its own innate rhythms, and often only needs space to work its own magic.

Assuming you would like to create the opportunities afforded by a discussion group, the first question is what type of group? "Discussion group" has been used as a generic term to cover a broad range of formats. Will it be a group to explore specific questions or themes? Is it a support group to talk through current life situations? Is it a very loosely structured, stream of consciousness rap group? Is it a consciousness-raising group with identified political, social or spiritual goals? Will the group be reading books or articles and then discussing them? Although they are valuable, I am not considering demos, lectures, or workshops of sexual technique and practice as discussion groups for the purpose of this essay. Workshops and demos may raise issues that can serve as good discussion topics, but a question/answer period does not a discussion make. The format should fit the purposes of the individual or group wishing to invest the significant amounts of time and energy required to sponsor a successful group. The plan for the group should also match the available resources and the available pool of participants. Who is the group intended for? Who is welcome? Must you be a member of an organization to join or is it open to the public? What level is the group aimed at—novices, old-timers or a mixture of both? Is this an open-ended group or are there a set number of discussions before the group begins again? Can people drop in and out of the discussions or does the group *close* after a certain point?

The identity of the sponsoring group or individual(s) helps to determine who will attend. An SM organization with a large mailing list and a diverse membership will probably attract a different group than a Backpatch club whose primary publicity was flyers at various bars and a more modest mailing. An unaffiliated individual announcing a discussion group in formation to meet in community center space or similar location will draw yet a different group. In distributing publicity about the group, please consider who the audience is for the publications or for locations used to distribute information. The reputation and the composition of the groups or individuals organizing the group will also help determine who will attend. Is this discussion group to be open to women and men? If that is the case, what steps will be taken to ensure a comfort level that will make gender balance a reality? Consideration of race, sexual orientation, and all the other forms of human identity differences and taking concrete steps to address the differences is essential to making a discussion group truly inclusive.

It may be that the purpose of the group calls for exclusivity, for separation. There is a powerful, potentially healing, atmosphere when a group is all women, all Gay, all African-American, all bottoms, all Tops, or all any other identity group. It is easier to build trust and disclose highly personal information in the company of others sharing comparable situations. The common knowledge of a homogeneous group also lessens the need to explain everything before getting to the heart of an exchange. There is also the danger of such a group becoming unhealthy. Every identity group has its frailties and blind spots. And although railing and raging is part of the healing process from societal hurts, bashing is another manifestation of illness. Focus on bashing the *other*, the enemy, is also a good way to avoid much needed discussions under the cover of staying within the bounds of the group's purpose. Before starting a discussion group ask yourself if the group is served by exclusivity and separation? If there are not clear and rational reasons directly related to the group's purpose for the exclusion of an individual or a class of individuals, then the separation is probably not founded on healthy motivations.

Regardless of the purpose of the group, it will have to be facilitated in some way. If you or someone in the sponsoring group already has group facilitation skills, you already have the most important ingredient. There is a popular belief in some communities that the responsibility of facilitating meetings should be rotated among the members of a group. The theory is that in so doing inequitable power arrangements are avoided and new people have a chance to spread their wings and develop skills. This may be a good practice for certain types of business or community meetings, but it has been my experience that it is a

117

bad idea with discussion groups. Unlike an organization, where the life of the group lies not in its business meetings but in its actions, the life of a discussion group *is* in the meeting. Whenever possible a person with experience should be used. I believe that having co-facilitators is a good practice. They can share the work, help to maintain continuity in a group, and if one is less experienced, the process of co-facilitating can be used as an apprenticeship. If an experienced person is unavailable, a group can still function if there is an agreed upon set of guidelines for the discussions and commitment to follow the guidelines.

Training in listening skills and basic group process is readily available through non-profit community organizations in exchange for volunteer time. This exchange of time for training benefits the individual receiving training, the discussion group, the non-profit agency, and the Kink community through bridge building and fostering good will. Increased visibility and participation by SM/Leather/Fetish people on hotlines, as care providers in HIV/AIDS organizations, and as active volunteers in other services will go a long way towards establishing real links between communities. The Kink community also benefits from the development of skills in community organizers who may then train others within the community. If you are planning on a consciousness raising group, I highly recommend the training materials available through the National Organization for Women, which can be modified easily.

Creating Safety

For there to be frank and open discussion, people must feel safe to speak their minds without fear of reprisal or a loss of privacy. One of the first and most important ground rules is that what is said in the group stays in the group. It may be helpful to start with a reminder about confidentiality. Even talking about what was shared minus names and identifying details reveal too much. It really is a small world. The SM/Leather/Fetish community is linked and intertwined in amazing ways, not the least of which is a fiber optic gossip net.

Safety also means freedom from personal attack. Although strong, intense debates and dialogues are a part of a healthy group, the attention must remain on ideas and behaviors and not on personalities. Merely setting this as a ground rule is generally not enough. If discussion becomes heated and crosses the line or is about to cross the line, call a time out. A pause to breathe, go to the bathroom, cool off, and loosen the grip of the moment can be helpful.

Over time a group may become frustrated by individuals in the group or by the feel of the group as a whole. Unacknowledged frustrations or disappointments can poison the atmosphere of a group. Periodically the group should schedule time to check in on these feelings and respond to them in constructive ways chosen by the group. Often several people will have similar frustrations that can be resolved through a little brainstorming. End these sessions with positive statements summarizing the discussions.

Encouraging Focus

Having a schedule of discussion topics and related questions is a simple and direct way to keep on track. If that seems too rigid, then try selecting the next theme or topic at the end of each group. Try to get word out to whoever might be attending the next group so that they come prepared. If there is a blackboard available use it to list the high points. It is the facilitator's responsibility to keep the group moving through the discussion: summing up or listing some of the points raised before moving on to the next part helps to give a sense of completion. Reminders about time are also relatively neutral ways to keep things moving. The agreed-upon time limit for a discussion should only be extended by the group, not the facilitator.

Consider making "I" statements the preferred mode of communication in the group. It is easy to avoid direct communication and accountability when speaking in the third person or in generalities. When someone starts their statement with "I" it reminds them that what they are about to say is their statement spoken with only their authority. Every statement in a group discussion can't be an "I" statement, but there is a strong correlation between a good group and the percentage of "I" statements made.

Having only one person speak at a time is a useful guideline, but often hard to follow. The facilitator can count off those people who are interested in speaking at any given point, and keep track of the queue. If this does not work, you may wish to try using a talking stick. Only the person holding the stick, shell, whip, or whatever object has been chosen, may speak and when they are done they pass it on to whomever is next.

Promoting Active Participation

Some people find it easier to speak in groups than others. To prevent a monopoly on air time, periodically ask a question that goes round the circle with the expectation that everyone will speak. After the question has made the full circle, go back and see if anyone who passed wishes to speak at that point. A variation of this can be used as a warm-up. Ask people to check in by saying their name and something that's happened to them recently they'd like to share.

For many people it is easier to speak in smaller groups, especially if discussing highly personal matters. Break the group up into twos or threes to discuss the question then reform the larger group to share observations. It's a good idea to suggest that people run things past their small group partners before sharing anything personal in the large group.

At the beginning of each discussion you may want to ask that everyone listen with undivided attention when someone is speaking. There are few times in daily life when we receive the gift of undivided attention and true listening from those around us. When offered that gift, many are willing to speak more fully and more directly from the heart. In and of itself, focused attention is a powerful tool to encourage participation.

Common Difficulties

Truth in advertising is always a good idea, but it is particularly important for discussion groups. Clear descriptions of the group's goals will help to gather appropriate people together and to limit disappointments based on false assumptions. If the group has open and closed periods for new members, you may wish to have discussion group demos so that people can sample the group before committing.

Struggles over the ownership or sponsorship should be avoided before a group begins. If it is sponsored by a club or organization that piece of information should be a part of all publicity for the group. If the facilitator for the group leaves, it is the sponsoring organization's responsibility to find a replacement. I have seen discussion groups take on a life of their own if neglected by their sponsor—which is fine if everyone is in agreement and the parting is amicable.

Intellectual competition and debates can be good if you are trying to create a forum for the refinement of ideas in the community, but can be deadly to discussion groups hoping to provide a space for personal development. Although this can be said of humans in general, egos are a big problem in the Kink community, and egos loom large in discussion groups. Assertive statements about ground rules, guidelines, and equal air time must be made when competitiveness begins to take over a group. If there are several people with a desire to debate community issues, then perhaps a forum should be established to fill that need.

In an effort to be sensitive, sometimes discussion groups fall prey to two of leatherphobia's more treacherous manifestations: pacification and accommodation. Working through the fears, doubts, and confusions related to integrating a SM/Leather/Fetish sexuality is usually very stressful. Sometimes members of discussion groups cannot bear the pain of someone else's distress, especially one so applicable to their own. They attempt to pacify or to calm the distressed person. They support the person in ways that do not help the person, but that do turn down the emotional volume in the group. It is also common for groups to accommodate fears or concerns by changing group policies, schedules, meeting locations, and so on in order to make someone more comfortable with the state of their closet.

Avoid boredom; over time some members will want more in-depth discussions than the mix of the group permits. Consider having a more advanced or more intensive group to fill these needs. For some people having a more advanced group available allows them to continue attending the more basic group because their needs are being better met, which frees up energy to spend on mentoring beginners. If you neglect these people, you also lose participants who may become facilitators for future groups.

It's Worth The Effort

That SM/Leather/Fetish sexualities are complex is indisputable. As a group, Kinky people are probably more diverse, containing more categories of significant difference than most other communities or identity groups. We are also one of the least understood and least explored of the sexual minority communities. It is almost universally acknowledged in our community that Kink is becoming more visible. With visibility comes new challenges and new questions. Where shall we find insights and answers? I believe that there is a strong case to be made for the limited utility, in fact the danger, of relying upon academia or the various professional communities for insights into the nature of the Kink community with its myriad of unique individuals. Until we have our own clear agenda and cultural manifesto, we must be wary of being done in by the *for their own good syndrome*. Discussion groups have the potential to be the wellspring for many of the ideas and insights that we need to develop our community. There will be many bad discussion groups, just as their are many bad relationships, but experience is often the wisest teacher. There will also be many groups that will serve as bright points of light, constant as the North star, to guide travelers and pilgrims on their journey of self -discovery.

Some Discussion Questions & Themes

• What do we mean by these words: pain, pleasure, sex, and play?

• If you are queer, what were the similarities and differences between coming out Queer and coming out Kink? If you are straight what was your experience of coming out and does it relate to what you've heard from the Queer people in the group?

• How do you feel when someone who is different from you (different gender, race, orientation, etc.) comes into your social space (bar, party, dungeon, etc.)?

• How do your spirituality and your religion relate to your sexuality? If you are agnostic or an atheist, how does your sexuality relate to your philosophy of life?

• What are the pros and cons of the Kink community becoming more visible, and less like a secret society? What are the potential conflicts and resolutions for individuals and groups with different beliefs about openness and secrecy?

• If you are a politically progressive person, how do you deal with the ideological criticism of Kink that is so prevalent? If you are politically conservative, how do you deal with the ideological criticism of Kink that is so prevalent at this time?

• How do you reconcile the illusions, images and mystique of the SM/Leather/Fetish community with the realities of your experiences?

• What are your ideas about monogamy, polyfidelity, open relationships, and everything in between?

• How does the leather title holder system help the community? How does it hurt the community? What other forms of leadership selection or recognition do we need?

• How are we doing at the business of building community. Are Bisexual, Pansexual, Straight, Lesbian, Gay, Transgendered all under the banner of Kink?

• Backpatch club, SM organization, GDI, and who knows what else. How many ways are there to organize and how can they all work together?

• Is substance abuse in the Kink community fostered by our over-reliance on bars, runs, beer busts, and other gatherings with a focus on alcohol? Why is the measure of a club's hospitality often how much liquor flowed?

• How does the SM/Leather/Fetish community support long term relationships? How does the community work against long term relationships?

• Is Kink a sexual orientation, a lifestyle, or something else? How does your sexual orientation relate to the SM/Leather/ Fetish part of your sexuality?

• How is feminism used against the Kink community? How can feminism help the Kink community?

• Who knows you're Kinky? Who do we trust with information about our sexuality? What are the benefits and the potential losses associated with self-disclosure?

• How do you discriminate against (other genders, races, orientations—pick one per discussion) in the Kink community? What can we do as individuals and as groups to lessen discrimination? Who is served by discrimination?

• What is a fetish? Where does the power of a fetish come from?

• What other movements or communities are our allies or potential allies? How should we build bridges to other communities?

• How do events in your life impact on your sexuality? Do you feel more Top or more bottom or are you attracted to certain things when life events take certain turns? How does power in your life affect power in the bedroom?

• What is butch? What is femme? What forms do sex roles take in leathersex?

• What are the difficulties and the strengths of mixed relationships (mixed in the sense of Kinky and non-Kinky)?

• Never in anger... how do we guard the lines between scenes, psychodrama, and abuse?

• How do we hold our media accountable? How do we deal with the mainstream media? With the Queer media?

• What do we want to see in the Kink community in five years, 10 years, and 20 years? What do we fear will be and what can we do about it?

• How do we tell our children about our sexuality? How can the Kink community responsibly look out for the needs of sexual minority youth?

• How has being a Kinky person enriched my life? What unique perspectives come from being a member of the SM/Leather/Fetish community? What perspectives do you bring to the Kink community from other communities you belong to?

• Top, bottom, and switch, what do these words mean to you?

• What do you call a person whose taste runs from very vanilla sex to rocky road? What do you call a person who only enjoys intense leathersex? Do we have concepts to cover the equivalent of a Hetero-Bi-Homo continuum for Kinky sexuality?

Introduction To The Shadow

Many psychologists, anthropologists, teachers of mythology or religion, and scholars use a concept called the *shadow* in making sense of the human condition. This is the shadow cast by the conscious mind and it contains those thoughts we repress. It also contains those feelings we drive out of our hearts. Although much of what is relegated to the shadow is ostensibly unhealthy or evil, good and healthy impulses and characteristics are consigned there because of personal fears or beliefs. In daily life, it is also common to speak of a dark side, a mean streak, or an alter-ego to express the idea that people have a part of themselves that is harsh, cruel, or animalistic. In ancient Egypt, Rome and other cultures, the shadows we cast, whether internal or external, were seen as parts of our souls that were precious and especially vulnerable. There are valid differences of opinion as to the nature of the shadow, but for the sake of the discussions in the three chapters that follow, I invite you to trace the shape of the shadow as I see it.

I believe that the shadow is more than a summation of all our flaws and negativity. The *shadow* is neither good nor evil but a part of ourselves that is mysterious, primal, and often unacceptable by the standards of mainstream society. All sane individuals have a shadow and all cultures and societies have their equivalent of a collective shadow. The dark parts of the self cannot be exorcised—only understood or accepted. Much of our personal power and vitality arises from our depths like the vigorous growth of plants fed from the dark decay of compost. To be whole is to recognize and to acknowledge the full span of identity.

For Leather people this is an especially arduous quest, but ultimately highly rewarding and essential to a balanced expression of sexuality. Much if not most of Kinky sexuality is the stuff that shadows are made of in this culture. The practitioners of radical sexual practices blur the lines drawn in society's sand, and those who choose black as the color of their attire, whether it be leather or lace, are visible reminders of the repressed shadow. The work of realizing or owning the shadow is difficult for everyone, but for those of us who are overshadowed by societal disapproval and by religious condemnation as well, the task is no less than Herculean. Often in the tumult of coming out as a Kinky person, fear and confusion overwhelm us and we drive away parts of our sexual selves that are essential to our health. It is a long, hard road for members of the SM/Leather/Fetish community to reclaim what is theirs.

This journey of self-discovery and self-healing is very private, with each individual finding their own path or creating it out of the wilderness of the inner landscape. Yet there are commonalities that we can share and moral and emotional support that can be offered. I have gained some understanding of my own shadow, and what I have learned I'll share.

The next chapter, "Scary Movies," offers an analysis of the phobias, the isms, the rhetoric, and the politics directed against Kinky people. It also suggests some of the ways that propaganda and oppression become internalized. "Possession" describes the damage done to us in this environment. When we internalize false images and beliefs from society we give up a certain amount of our free will. To the degree that we internalize someone else's shadow we have less energy to proceed with our own personal growth, and often add the burden of outright interference. "Soul Retrieval" is about claiming our own true dark with all its strength and weakness. It is about liberation from the shame and fear generated by external perspectives on our community. Leather sexuality in its healthy expression becomes a vehicle for personal wholeness and integration.

If you don't have a spiritual or philosophical bent, you might be tempted to stop here and settle for the essays which seem more immediately interesting or useful—please don't. The examples and images you'll find in this section on the shadow are about real life and concrete situations. I believe that most readers will find their own dark reflection in these chapters, because however different and diverse we may be we all have a shadow.

Scary Movies

No doubt you've had the experience of a friend vigorously criticizing or complaining about someone else's behavior or attitudes, and have smiled to yourself that the criticisms and complaints were an apt description of that very friend's failings. When a person chooses to see their own faults in other people, rather than in themselves, the person is engaging in projection. Although it can be a cause for amusement in some settings, the results of projection can be incredibly damaging. This is especially true when not only minor foibles are being projected, but also parts of the individual or collective shadow. Projection is a common way for individuals and for cultures to deny their own problems and to use other individuals or groups such as minorities as scapegoats. Projection is one of the ways stereotypes are built up or elaborated upon. Some small characteristic, cue, or kernel of truth in a minority becomes the peg upon which many falsehoods and fears can be hung. In truth this can happen with any identifiable grouping of people whether they are the majority or a minority. The impact of the stereotyping then depends upon the balance of social power and the level of psychological health and maturity of the communities in question. If the image that is projected onto individuals belonging to a minority is very strong then they become very hard to see through the projection. One of the classic symptoms of *isms* (like sexism, racism, etc.) is perceiving the other, the minority, as a monolithic grouping with less individual variation. That is, individuals become generalities.

Something human history has proven without a doubt is that when we cease to see others as individuals with unique characteristics we are more capable of doing them harm. It is generally emotionally easier for a soldier to press a button and fire a long-range missile than it is for him to drop a bomb from a plane, and more difficult yet to shoot a gun when you can see the eyes of the person in your sights. Unfortunately, this continuum of an increase in humane behavior as the context becomes more personal breaks down under the influence of projected shadows. The stronger the emotional, psychological, and psychic power of the projection the less of the individual is visible or perceivable at any range. The images projected upon Kinky people are laser-sharp portrayals that deindividualize and dehumanize, even go so far as to demonize.

People in the Leather/SM/Fetish communities, through the mere act of expressing rather than repressing their identities, put into motion a complex net of societal antagonism. Those pursuits that are the joy and the heart of the Kink community challenge the criteria that the majority of Western culture uses to determine what is acceptable and what is not. Here we find a basic parting of ways between communities and ultimately between worldviews. This parting is not amicable because the mainstream claims ownership over those people who are avowing a distinctly different identity. Speaking simplistically, this means that white men are seen as traitors to society when they live differently from the straight and narrow idol set before them, and for everyone else the claiming of another way of being marks an increase in deviance and a potential for rebellion. As individuals and as cultures we dish out disapproval and punishment in many different flavors, with different presentations, depending upon our relationship to the person and to our respective groupings and affiliations. Much has been said in Progressive and Feminist circles about the dangers of the objectification of people, and of the greater health of subject/subject relationships as opposed to subject/object relationships. While there may be some truth in this assumption, when it comes to the enforcement of societal norms, a subject/subject relationship may actually increase the ferocity of the attempt to bring a person into compliance.

Because we come in an almost infinite mixture of possible combinations of characteristics such as gender, race, class, sexual orientation, religion, etc. the lines between us that determine us/them, subject/object, minority/majority and so on lose their clarity. The lines may blur, or become shapes rather than lines, with an enormous increase in the complexity of possible interactions and relationships. Bring to your mind the image of an upper class Heterosexual Leatherwoman, an African-American Gay Leatherman, a middle class White Bisexual Leatherwoman, and as many other people as you'd like to imagine, and explore the many shapes that privilege, power, and prejudice can take. In other essays in this book the power and the beauty of diversity has been celebrated, so don't despair—but this section is on the shadow.

In seeking the roots of oppression and the factors that decide what is of the shadow (unacceptable) and what is of the light (acceptable), many stop at the base of the tree trunk and declare it the beginning. Many ascribe economics, political power, or other similar factors as the root causes of our social woes, but these merely shape the methods and the means of oppression. To find the roots you must go below the surface into the darkness of the soil. Beneath the surface you find the beliefs, the worldviews, and the images that feed and support both the healthy and unhealthy branches of our cultural tree. Much of what we find in this metaphorical soil is religion, philosophy, and the needs of the spirit. The mainstream culture has a profound dislike for the body, bodily functions and the physical world that springs from a religious and philosophical history that splits mind from body and spirit from matter. Those who deny the body and the physical world are seen as holy and those who immerse themselves in the world are seen as profane. This cultural condemnation of the physical world that we live in is at odds with the very real desires that people feel and with the pleasures derived from experiences in the world. This conflict, this dissonance, causes shame, discomfort, and the repression of genuine feelings and needs that then become part of the shadow of individuals and societies. This is projected upon others. Kinky people indulge in and enjoy sensuality in its sweetest and in its most pungent forms. Virtually everything of the body from menstrual flow to piss to pubic musk, is *someone's* delight. Almost anything from a boot to a braided whip to a wisp of red silk can be endowed with the glow of sensual pleasure in the eye of the right beholder.

Our society is also filled with the abuse and misuse of force, power, and hierarchy. There are conflicting political and psychological perspectives on the nature of power in our society, but there is a general acknowledgment that something is terribly wrong. There are conflicting messages that both vilify and honor aggressive behavior. There are conflicting messages that both encourage and denounce assertive behavior. From the moment, early in life, when we gain an awareness of individual identity and of our interdependence upon others we struggle with the balance of autonomy and shared control of the outcome of the events in our daily lives. Images of violence and of overt power often appear in the minds of gentle citizens who quickly push them into the furthermost cubbyholes of their brains. Others do not even allow the images to surface for a moment, and have a silent guardian standing at the threshold of their conscious mind denying admission to all images not meeting the cultural dress code. Here, once again, the personal and collective shadow grows larger. This is projected upon others. Often Kinky people take the images of power and elaborate upon them, expand them, and build up a scene that takes the base leaden material of violence and turns it into the Alchemical gold of power.

The first question, the most often asked question, at the birth of a child is not, "Is the child healthy?" but rather "Is it a boy or a girl?." Gender, and all the constructs and the realities that spring from it such as gender identities, sex roles, and sexual orientations are at the foundation of most societies and form the basic outlines of the identities that people are encouraged and trained to claim. Sexism, Misogyny, Misandry, Heterosexism, and Homophobia are some of the enforcers of societal strictures.

134

Denial of feelings and needs that do not fit into the mainstream norm and their attendant fears and self-hatred become part of the shadow. This is projected upon others. Many Kinky people play with gender and roles as loosely and as freely as a child with fingerpaint.

Now this collective shadow has grown large, and it does not fit neatly into its assigned compartments. It is so large that at times it spills out and becomes visible—completely unacceptable since the shadow is everything whose sight cannot be tolerated. An attempt is then made to cast it away, the further the better, past the boundaries of the social map, that map being the shape and the form of the mainstream society. Ancient map makers knew well what they did in placing the dragons and the monsters past the edge of the civilized world. Those people practicing radical sexualities are at or beyond the edge of the social map, and hence are prime candidates to become the screens upon which the shadows are cast. A curious property of shadows in the physical world is that the further they are cast the larger and the more distorted they become. This property holds true in the realms of the mind and the spirit. When the shame, fear, anger, unmet hungers, and confusion arising from inner conflict and ambivalence over the body, sexuality, power, and identity take the form of projected shadows, the shapes and images are monstrous indeed.

Anything that is different or unknown is often the target of prejudice. The sexual practices, relationship styles, and social norms of Kinky people are different from and generally unknown to most of mainstream society, and that alone would be enough to generate oppressive actions, but there is more. Leather/SM/Fetish sexualities play with power, revel in the myriad forms of the body and all its functions, play with roles, blur, bend, and redefine identities, acknowledge that spirit is housed in a body, and indulge in pleasure/pain for its own sake. Where else but the Kink community would these shadows be projected? When people project their shadows onto Leather people they experience many things, two of which are especially important. One: their ability to see the person underneath the overlay of their shadow is greatly hampered. Two: they feel the emotions associated with their own unacceptable selves and they wish to punish or destroy those people wearing the shape of their shadow. Both of these speak to why the Kink community is often attacked by the Religious Right, declared pathological by so-called mental health practitioners, and used as a bogey man by many.

Ironically and sadly, the harder and farther individuals or cultures try to push away their shadows the larger, more looming, and more frightening they become. Because no one can outrun their shadow, there is a building desperation that can become a vicious circle leading to greater and greater levels of polarization and escalating hostilities. As the Kink community has become more visible in the world (an affirming and healthy action in my estimation) there has been a sharp increase in overt attacks, discriminations and reprisals. There are many reasons for this change, not the least of which is that greater visibility means more targets and more clear shots, but also that we are breaking fundamental rules, including the rule of silence and shame. There are few affronts greater, to people of a certain mindset, than communicating in word or in deed that societal approval is not needed to justify the truth of your body and your spirit. There may also be redirected resentment because the Kink community is doing (or is believed to be doing) those things that individuals and cultures would like to do but are prevented from doing by their own self-censure. Openness also generates fear because what they see when they look upon the Kink community is not the actual living community with its failings and successes, but the monstrous image of their projected shadow. There is also outrage because the monster has left its appointed place and has stepped onto the social map. The dragons have left their ghetto.

Unfortunately, we left our ghetto trailed not only by our own shadows, but by those pinned upon us like a donkey's tail, and by the shadows of the shadows projected upon us. Kinky people like all people have their own shadow, have internalized their part of the collective shadow, and have also projected their shadows upon others. Additionally, the shadows projected upon Kinky people have been internalized, creating shadows upon shadows.

Possession

Whether surveyed from the vantage point of psychology, spirituality, or the elusive principle of common sense, it is known that a lie repeated often enough has the force of truth. Further, the more complete the lie the more power it assumes. To some degree we judge reality by its construction; we equate richness of detail and context with the probability of truth. In judging someone's testimony the distinction between perjury and truth is often the ability to flesh out the bare bones of a story and to speak with conviction. There is no doubt in my mind that the Religious Right, and others of their ilk, have carefully crafted a full world view and a mythology that use Kinky people as its negative polarity. More dangerous than the dogmas, rationales and politics are the mythic images arising from their world view and their shadows.

The shadows projected upon Kinky people do not stay on the surface. The psychic skin, like physical skin, is a permeable boundary, so each of us, according to our own natures, absorb a certain amount of our surroundings. Lest we bog down in this metaphor, please bear in mind that in the case of our psychic surroundings what is being absorbed are images, emotions, mythic themes, and ideas that unlike material things may multiply, combine, metamorphose, and change in dimension or volume—freely flaunting the limits of the physical. Once the projected shadows have crossed the boundary that divides the outside world from our inner world, those shadows become subject to the rules of our psychological natures. The projected shadows are identified as shadows, and as such are relegated to those places in the psyche that are our personal underworld. As in many other instances, it is our defenses that become our enemy, and our beliefs that provide the enemy with the shape for our personalized Trojan horse.

Our culturally ingrained defenses will argue that so long as we keep a clear head and examine a situation or a lie rationally, we need not be trapped by false assertions. To a degree that is so, but only a degree. It is possible to argue away the attacks made by the Religious Right and Fundamentalists on the place of Kinky people in society through the recourse of civil liberties litigation, the invocation of the social value of tolerance and privacy in a pluralistic society, and commentary on the dangers of religious extremism. It is possible to feel a righteous anger when viewing propaganda depicting leather people as slavering fiends, and to know intellectually that image is a falsehood. What the rationalism that fetters us can't do is prevent those images from seeping into our souls. We are ill-prepared to safely ground our anger in action, or to comfort away the fears, but perhaps the most hazardous flaw we inherit from the common culture is the reticence to look the shadow in the eye.

Once the shadow that has been projected upon us is internalized it does not stay dormant. It has as free a rein in our dark chasms as our own shadows have. It is also safely beyond the net of rationality and logic, and it has an advantage. There is a balance in our internal ecology of thoughts, images, emotions, and sensations that has been with us since birth and evolves and adapts over the course of our lives. A foreign shadow introduced into our inner ecology has the advantage of the gypsy moth, of kudzu, of rabbits in Australia, of Dutch Elm disease—it has no natural checks or balances save perhaps one. Our own personal shadows understand the nature of the projected/internalized shadows, and so develop the capacity to control them. However, it is uncommon for people in modern cultures to be in touch with their shadow, so that recourse is not generally available.

In fact, to the degree that a person has alienated or rejected their personal shadow there will be a corresponding possibility that their shadow will join forces with the foreign shadow. The person's shadow invites the intruder across the threshold and bares their imaginary neck. This alliance results in what I consider to be possession. This may seem an extreme term that calls up images of B-grade horror movies, but I believe it to be an apt description. Possession can be defined as being controlled or influenced by external and antagonistic beings or forces— certainly applicable in this case. Possession also implies acting in a manner that is not faithful to an individual's true self or being prevented from acting in a genuine way. In Dr. Carl G. Jung's theoretical work, will was the amount of available psychic energy that could be directed or shaped by conscious intent for any given purpose. Its availability for use is determined by how free the individual is from distorted or hidden patterns. A person who is possessed has limited free will and is certainly caught in a snare of distortion and lies. Although it is only anecdotal evidence, I have heard people in the SM/Leather/Fetish community speak of times when they have been overwhelmed by a rush of actions and emotions wherein they were unwilling spectators within their own bodies. This sounds like possession to me, and it is not the same as surrendering to your own true passions and needs, though on the surface the two may appear similar. A brilliant and revealing glimpse of some of this dark dynamic and its resolution can be found in Gabrielle Antolovich's essay in the *Leatherfolk* anthology. If you have neither personally experienced this state of being nor have had a friend recount their experience, I strongly recommend you read Antolovich's essay and begin to ask your friends and yourself questions about your free will.

Unlike Hollywood's representation of possession, the real thing is no absolute dive into green vomit-spouting oblivion; rather it is varying shades that tinge the individual's character and behavior. Nonetheless it can be dramatic. An acquaintance I met at school went through two transformations that were dramatic and illustrative of this type of possession. When I first met him he was ostensibly a straight jock, a bulked up football player, with such good defenses that my *gaydar* had not even spotted him as potentially queer. He eventually came out as a Gay man and in the course of a few weeks became a stereotype in the flesh. His walk, his talk, and his mannerisms were cliche perfection. His makeup, earrings, stick-pin, and cowl neck sweater were flawless. Don't mistake me, there is nothing wrong with playing with gender and claiming a unique expression of your combination of female and male qualities however you define them. There was nothing genuine in this young man's presentation—he wasn't becoming himself, he was becoming the *faggot* his parents had warned him about. Needless to say, there were a number of painful incidents generated by this sudden transformation, in part because of heterosexism and in part because he was not acting from his true self. The disruptions in his life led him to leave the area. When I saw him again, years later, he'd become a vision of black leather severity. He'd come out into SM and had once again been transformed into the *pervert* that his parents had warned him about. He was cruel, harsh, and predatory in the way of someone who believed themselves damned. I was appalled, and at the time did not understand how or why this had happened. I did not make an effort to maintain contact with him, but ours is a small world so I did run into him again. I was heartened to discover that he'd become a whole person; he liked himself and in turn was very much like the big likable lug I'd first met years ago.

He'd also stopped drinking, which played no small part in his health and happiness. The roots of addiction are many and individual, but I do believe that if part of a person's will has been commandeered by an internalized shadow, they are much more susceptible to substance abuse. The desire to auto-sedate is great if you are becoming or behaving as a stranger to your self, and the internalized shadow, the self-destroyer, will encourage the use of substances that erode the personality. The higher proportion of sexual minorities with substance abuse problems, as compared to the general population, is also related to the stress of oppression, lowered self-esteem, and the large percentage of social venues that are substance-based such as bars and runs. However, the spiritual and inner aspects of being Kinky or a sexual minority should not be underrated in considering addiction and recovery. Self-abuse or addictive behavior can take other forms, including but not limited to the misuse of sex, food, and relationships.

There are many less dramatic but equally harmful forms of possession. Lesser grades can take the form of the inner tormentor that speaks words of fear and shame into your inner ear. The tormentor may put butterflies in your stomach, paint your palms with cold sweat or freeze you with emotional numbness like a demonic Jack Frost. The tormentor may replay images in your head of a firebombed bookstore or community center as you go out for the evening, or recall the latest article in the paper describing a bashing. The tormentor may whisper doubts that drive you to push away potential lovers. Indeed, we all harbor the seeds of self-sabotage, just as we harbor the seeds of hope. What I'm suggesting is that it is one thing to deal with your *own* issues and quite another to deal with interloping neuroses. The more technically-minded might consider these to be like computer viruses, Trojan horses, and worms. Or you could look at this like an Orwellian horror where Big Brother is everywhere including inside your head, and speaking to you in your own voice. Or as a mean spirited shade that lurks within looking to tarnish every silver lining.

People differ in psychological and spiritual stamina. Some are able to continue on the path of their choice while dragging the kicking and screaming tormentor behind them. They could move faster if they were unburdened. Others crawl or are brought to a dead stop by the burden and the resistance of the internalized shadow. Some find that they expend so much of their will, their free psychic energy, on treading in the emotional waters that they make no headway in the integration of their Kink with the rest of their self concept. No matter how strong an individual may be or may become the internalized shadow matches their strength, like a leech drawing its strength from the person it afflicts. Like a leech it must be removed; running doesn't help.

If the internalized shadow, the shadow shaped by the fears and the hatreds of those who despise sexual difference, is not dealt with, the person at the very least becomes spiritually anemic. Often in extremity there is clarity. In J.R.R. Tolkien's *Lord of the Rings*, unfortunates such as Gollum and the Ring Wraiths bear an evil, a spiritual malaise, so much greater in scope than their own individualities that they are eaten away until they more closely match the image of evil than themselves. The idea that we are the Religious Right's picture of their *Dorian Gray* is another way to imagine the projected shadow. Unlike literature, real life is hardly so coherent and so clear cut, but there is a lesson to be learned nonetheless. We can become drained of our vital force. We can feel hollow and the sweet taste of life can become ashes in our mouths if we do not clear out the propaganda, the lies, the internalized shadows that delight in our downfall.

Soul Retrieval

One of the common ills in modern life is the sensation of being bereft of something important. For some this is a boredom, an ennui, that is often masked by risk taking, substance abuse, or other forms of escape or sedation. This loss can be experienced as a lack of purpose or meaning. It can be described as feeling empty or soul-less. When our sexual selves have been marginalized or to some degree relegated to the shadow there is a profound sense of loss. Our capacity for joy, ecstasy, and satisfaction is diminished when we have lost a part of our shadow. This lost part of the self is actually buried deep within—the loss is a loss of access. Many ancient and some living indigenous cultures have developed a more sophisticated grasp of the human psyche than is usually held in the common knowledge of Western industrialized society.

A shaman or a spiritual healer would look upon this malaise of emptiness or apathy with understanding, empathy, and a definite course of action. There is a healing practice, known by many names, to reunite the estranged parts of the self. Soul retrieval is one of the more descriptive names for this healing, and one that is meaningful in the context of the shadow and of possession. Regardless of your personal stance on matters of the spirit or of psychology, I believe that this metaphor, this model, can be adapted for your use or can offer insights into the integration of the primal parts of Kink sexual identity.

When a shaman or healer perceives a certain type of illness or emptiness they say that the person has lost their soul. They say that the soul is confused, wandering or has been stolen. It is possible for the foreign shadow that has been internalized to hold the personal shadow hostage. The banishing of a part of yourself, as with the shadow, appears to be a modern illness that would have confounded the wisest of medicine people. It should be noted that the spirit is not the same as the soul. There is often a distinction made between the spark of the collective eternal that can never be lost, and the soul which is the essence of the individual. The healer and/or the person to be healed go on inner journeys through dreams, trances, visualizations, or pathworkings to find what has strayed, been banished or stolen, and bring it home. When it is brought home it is blown back into the center of the person, often through the place on the top of the head that was the soft round parting of the skull in infancy. Sometimes the soul that has been brought back must be appeased or convinced to remain. This approach may seem irrational or impossible, but methods refined over the centuries often work whether or not the mechanism of their action is understood. It should also be remembered that the language that is understood by the unconscious, the subconscious, the preconscious, and however else the non-linear parts of the self are labeled, is not words but images. The shadow, as we have defined it in these discussions, certainly contains vital parts of the soul, parts of the self. Under the influence of mainstream culture we are likely to banish it, as surely as some parts of the culture would like to banish us. We internalize their desire to make us go away. If that isn't a curse, I don't know what a curse is.

It may be that the course you take to retrieve those lost parts of the soul may be similar to that of traditional shamanism. If that is your choice, find someone who is trained in shamanism; it is a powerful technique with risks as well as benefits. It may be that keeping a journal of your dreams and impressions will provide you with the key to unlock the door. It may be that therapeutic work through a counselor or a discussion group will serve to place a candle of welcome in the window to your deep inner expanses. For those with the good fortune of trusted sexual partners, much healing can take place on the stage of sexual play. For those who can go the distance, intense sexual play can be like a journey through the soul's night country. People who live in their thoughts more than their feelings may have to discover and adopt a philosophy that has a place for the primal in its scheme of things. The ways towards personal wholeness are many, and only you can discern which is best for you. Whichever approach or combination of approaches you may take, it is important to remember to have patience. Progress usually comes in small increments, and only once in a great while is there an epiphany, a leap forward.

Finding those lost parts of the self is only the first step in the process. Once found they must be convinced to return and to remain. For integration to occur there must be peacemaking, which means trust and appreciation for that which was so unacceptable as to be cast out. It means looking your hidden desires in the eye and trusting that you can find a positive and creative way to express them. It means trusting in your own basic goodness enough to respond to yourself with compassion and control, even if what you see is absolutely counter to many of your cherished values and beliefs. It means having the will to take the raw polarities of dominance and submission, of passive and active, and of force and form, and to shape them into interaction and not violence. It means knowing that you want to live, to prevail at the same time that you are courting the lightening strike of a powerful experience. Perhaps most importantly, it is also the humility to offer credit and honor to the vitality that comes from the shadow. Offering thanks is the surest sign of appreciation and atonement.

Borrowing once again from the wisdom of elder cultures, each of us has an animal self, sometimes several animals. The animal part of our natures can be expressed symbolically as power animals, our allies, or as dangerous beasts, our adversaries. Because of the devaluation of the natural in our culture the shadow often contains a good part of our animal nature, or animal soul. Kink sexuality has the potential to be a union of the animal, the human, and the divine. Sadly this potential to be a bridge spanning the realms of being is rarely achieved. One sign that the animal component of Kink still retains vitality is in the common use of imagery containing eagles, bears, pigs, wolves, and composite beings such as griffins, satyrs, and centaurs in the iconography of our community. Another sign is the power that we recognize in smell, sight, touch, the sensory appreciation of life. When the smell of leather sends hot and cold rushes through our bodies, it is the animal responding. The response may be shaped by cultural associations but the saddle should not be confused with the horse. Whether top, bottom, or whatever other role has been taken, it is the animal self that most clearly understands the truth of the body. The animal self makes possible the amazing feats involved in some SM/Leather/Fetish practices. To have peace with our shadow we must reconcile the animal needs and desires with the human needs and desires. If not, then the trapped animal will chew off its leg to escape or grow hostile in its cage. We must recognize that we are maimed or that we fill with rage, when our animal self is mistreated. The animal part of the shadow must be coaxed back.

The human part of the shadow must also be reclaimed, but unlike the animal self it will not be pure and straight-forward. The human part of the shadow contains hopes, fears, and complicated needs. The lost longings, powerlessness, and despotic rages of our child self are there. The perceived inadequacies and failures of the adolescent are there. The sorrow, the doom, and the regret of the adult are there. Capitulations and surrender to the limitations of society and culture are there, but so too are the power of rebellion and individuation. The human part of the shadow wants to change the world as much as the animal must affirm it. This is the part of the shadow that tends to be most easily fragmented and distorted by the mainstream culture. It also responds most quickly to changes brought about by adopting a new set of cultural values and guidelines. The building of a stable Kink community and culture would help dramatically in reclaiming this part of the shadow.

Only when progress has been made in reclaiming the personal shadow can the removal of foreign shadow begin. The shadow of society's fears and hates that has been internalized becomes interwoven with our personal shadow. To be effective in disentangling the two requires that we be able to identify what is valuable and what is not. This is a potentially painful process but Kinky people are no strangers to the magic of transforming pain into satisfaction and accomplishment. The internalized shadow will fight for its survival, for the energy that it has leeched away. It will use tools such as illusion, mis-direction, self-doubt, and self-hate so it is often wise to seek counsel from professionals or peers in order to retain balance. True mental and spiritual health is a subtle blend of inner and outer harmony which, among other things, means having identity in the context of community. Another reason it is important to reconnect with the personal shadow before removing the foreign shadow is that nature abhors a vacuum. As fast as the internalized shadow is pushed out, something new, foreign, and toxic will fill the gap—unless the personal shadow is ensconced in its rightful place.

For you brave souls who may not have a metaphysical bent, and have read this far, I ask that you consider again the shadow, the power of possession, and soul retrieval as fables, as allegories that may correspond to your political philosophies. Oppression whether external or internal is too large to be *held* or *beheld* by anyone. The magnitude of oppression, both in the small interplay of details or in vast overarching connections, is as impossible to hold in the conscious mind as it is to visualize the number one thousand, let alone one million. Scholar and wizard Joseph Campbell once described the spiritual as comparable to a fragrance that arises from the material. Our imaginative capabilities can extract the quintessence of truth from the overwhelming mass of experience. Just as our eyes and our nervous system condense a torrent of photons into the thin stream of vision that the mind can comprehend, symbols and stories make human life more comprehensible. Myth takes the broad flood of life and fits it to the stream of our consciousness.

Politically it may be useful to deconstruct societal structures and norms to break chains and cycles of oppression, but deconstruction must be followed by construction or nothing but destruction will result. Reductionism has never brought new vitality to the world. Myth and imagination are indispensable to humanity: we need both bread and roses. It is my belief that if we reclaim our own true dark, we will have an unprecedented explosion of personal growth and vitality. The energy that has been locked up as self-oppression will be converted to political action, community building, and love. I haven't a clue as to what new vistas will open to us when we are whole, but I have faith that they exist. It is my hope that we in the Kink community will clench tight in our fists the thorny leather rose that is also our blazing golden bough, lighting a path to a future of our own choosing.

Epilogue

The SM/Leather/Fetish community is expanding and diversifying as we become freer and as we establish more and more venues for social interaction. This change offers opportunities for unity and for division. In the past, one of the strongest forces keeping the community unified was its small size. We did not have the luxury of separation nor was it advisable to muddy the waters of the communal well. Despite being scattered by great distances, there was a small-town quality to our interactions, even in urban areas. It only required a bit of brainstorming to find that we were friends of friends of friends or that we had ex-lovers of ex-lovers in common, or had come out into leather at the same bar, or had some other faint but real connection. Now, this net of connections has been spread thin. We are so many and so open to claiming our unique affinities that we are dividing into specialized cultures within cultures. Many of these can only survive in the hothouse climate of the largest of urban centers. Most of these new cultural units are insular, parochial, isolationist. Their disconnection from the Kink community as a whole is in direct proportion to how appealingly complete they are in their world views, roles, and identities.

We have lost the binding force of being small and being confined to a small set of choices as individuals and as communities. It is possible in this larger Kink universe to be anonymous within the context of community; you need not be a member of a tribe to get basic needs met. It is possible to move from geographical area to area as an escape from dealing with the responsibilities of being a member of a community. It is possible for people belonging to specific cultural units, such as Backpatch clubs, or fetish affinities, or the less formal but real society of fisters, to view the rest of the Kink community with

151

only marginal interest. Gone with the *small* days are the surety and the comfort of particular symbols, codes of dress, and codes of behavior meaning more or less the same thing to members of the Kink community. From certainty to probability to slight possibility, the hope of finding a kindred spirit when encountering a fellow Kinky person has diminished. The disappointment experienced in these circumstances is often one more wedge placed between us.

Are we a nation of tribes? I hope so, but that will only become a reality when we recognize the force that unites us. A good part of what held us together in the past was the force of oppression. To our credit we have broken the lock to that cage, but now that we are out of our cultural cage and free to risk the great outdoors—how will we remain together? I believe it is a matter of politics but also of spirituality. We can and will disagree on what needs to be done to establish social, economic, and political justice for Kinky people and how to go about it. How the struggle to move forward as a united community will play out depends on whether we view each other as parts of the same *people* or as unrelated allies. The sense of being the same tribe or people is a matter of the heart and of the spirit, because it means believing that we spring from the same deep wellspring of life.

If we view ourselves as a people, a tribe, a community we will make different choices in our interactions and relationships. No one and nothing is disposable or valueless if it is a member of the tribe. If there is illness in the body politic, healing is what is required, and amputation is the last recourse, not the first. So long as we recognize that we are interconnected then we are more likely to act in kind and appropriate ways. I have hope that we will recognize the intrinsic patterns of connection that make us a community. If we allow ourselves to unfold in a natural and organic manner, I believe that the dramatic growth we are experiencing will be a coming of age rather than an uncontrolled cancer. The health of a community is the summation of the health of its individuals. Each of us must begin with ourselves and the choices we make in how we treat others.

It may seem a daunting task, a hopeless task, for an individual to presume to make a difference, but that is where all differences begin. There is a Zen story that has always given me hope that I'd like to share. A Zen Master and a discouraged student are walking together along the shore of a lake. The Master asks the student to pick up a pebble and throw it into the lake. The student does so, and is asked to observe the lake. The Master then asks him if it has changed. The puzzled student finally answers that there is no difference. The Master explains that though they cannot see it, be assured that the level of the lake has risen. Trust in the weight of the pebble.

ABOUT THE AUTHOR

Ivo Domínguez, Jr. has been an activist in several movements and communities since 1976, his awakening to social action coinciding with his coming out as a Gay man. He was active with the Lesbian, Gay, Bisexual Student Union at the University of Delaware, helped to found the Gay and Lesbian Alliance of Delaware, served on Wilmington Delaware's Civil Rights Commission as its Vice-Chair and first openly gay person, he was one of the founding members of the Delaware Coalition for Lesbian, Gay & Bisexual Rights and served on the Board of the National Gay & Lesbian Task Force. He devoted him primary focus to AIDS/HIV work for nine years helping to found Delaware Lesbian & Gay Health Advocates, and served as its first Executive Director. He also served on the State of Delaware's AIDS Advisory Task Force and the Medical Society of Delaware's Blue Ribbon AIDS Commission. He and his lover owned and managed Hen's Teeth, Delaware's first alternative bookstore that served as a crossroads and common ground for many communities. He has been active in the Kink community since 1982, working most recently with the 1993 March on Washington's SM/Leather/Fetish Contingent. He was one of the founders of the Griffins MC, and has presented on Kink issues at the National Lesbian and Gay Health Foundation's conferences. He is also a Wiccan Priest within the Assembly of the Sacred Wheel, and is active in the Neo-Pagan community. He is continuing in his involvement with various movements, with his writing, and with life.

Available from Daedalus Publishing Company

BOOKS

Leathersex
A Guide for the Curious Outsider and the Serious Player

Everyone wants a more interesting and fulfilling erotic life. With that in mind, this book was written to give guidance to one popular style of erotic play which the author calls "leathersex"—sexuality that may include S/M, bondage, dominance, submission, fantasy, role playing, sensual physical stimulation, and fetish, to name just a few. The reader will find much wisdom between these covers about this often misunderstood form of erotic expression. If you are simply curious about leathersex, or if you already enjoy its pleasures but want to learn more, this book is for you. Price: $14.95

Ties That Bind
The SM/Leather/Fetish Erotic Style
Issues, Commentaries and Advice

The writings of one of the most respected and knowledgeable people on the subject of the SM/leather/fetish erotic style has been compiled in this book. Issues regarding relationships, the community, the SM experience, and personal transformation, as they relate to this form of erotic play, are addressed. The author, Guy Baldwin, is a well-known psychotherapist whose clients include many men and women who engage in this form of erotic play. Unlike many in the mental health field, Mr. Baldwin takes the approach that this style of erotic play can definitely be part of a healthy expression of one's sexuality. Many have benefited from his sound advice in seminars, workshops, and through his many published articles. Now, much of this man's wisdom has been published for you in this book. Price: $14.95

Learning the Ropes
A Basic Guide to Safe and Fun S/M Lovemaking

Curious about S/M? Perhaps you have always had an interest but did not know where to find reliable information. Or perhaps you just want to enhance your lovemaking with a spouse or partner. Whatever your reason for an interest in S/M, this book can help. This concise book guides the reader through the basics of safe and fun S/M. Learn what S/M is, how to do it safely, and how to connect with partners, plus much more. Written by S/M expert Race Bannon. Destined to become a classic in its field. Price: $12.95

The Master's Manual
A Handbook of Erotic Dominance

The idea of erotically dominating a partner appeals to many men and women. Unfortunately, there have been few resources from which to learn how to do this in a safe, fun, and responsible way. Now there is *The Master's Manual*. Author Jack Rinella examines various aspects of erotic dominance including SM, safety, sex, erotic power, techniques, and much more. Even if your primary interest is erotic submission rather than dominance, this book will give you insights that will help lead you to a more fulfilling sexuality. The author speaks in a clear, frank, and nonjudgmental way to any man or woman, regardless of sexual orientation, with an interest in the erotic dominant/submissive dynamic. Price: $14.95

Beneath The Skins
The New Spirit And Politics Of The Kink Community
In recent years, large numbers men and women have coalesced into a vibrant community that generally refers to itself as the leather/SM/fetish community. This community is defined by a common interest in styles of sexuality that are broadly described by the term "leather/SM/fetish." With the emergence of this fledgling community, as with any other, struggles to delineate common goals, definitions and political agendas are inevitable. This book examines such issues in a forum that, from the start, embraces the concept that people may truly define themselves and the community to which they belong by their erotic orientations and preferences. This special community is coming of age, and this book helps to pave the way for all who are part of it. Price: $12.95

The Leather Contest Guide
A Handbook for Promoters, Contestants, Judges and Titleholders
This is truly the complete guide to the leather contest. Contest promoters, contestants, judges and winners will all benefit from the sound advice presented in this book. Written by Guy Baldwin, one of the most famous names in the leather community and a former titleholder, this book clearly details the keys to a successful leather contest. Even those in the audience will enjoy the insights this book will give about the world of the leather contest. Price: $12.95

OTHER PUBLICATIONS

The S/M Resources Guide
Where do you find S/M equipment stores, mail order suppliers, leather craftspeople, S/M-oriented books and magazines, computer bulletin boards catering to the S/M community, S/M clubs and organizations, lists of S/M community events, or anything else related to your S/M interests? Now you can turn to The S/M Resources Guide. This guide is updated regularly, sometimes daily, and supplied to you in photocopied form so that you will have the most current information possible. Price: $9.95

How to Make Rope Restraints
Leather wrist and ankle restraints are common toys used during S/M play. But these types of restraints are expensive and don't always fit comfortably. Race Bannon has developed these instructions for making a set of rope restraints that function much like the more expensive leather restraints, but with more versatility and comfort. Rope restraints are comfortable, inexpensive, and will adjust to any size wrist or ankle. With these instructions, and a few dollars worth of rope, you can construct a set of four restraints in just minutes. Price: $3.95

ORDERING INFORMATION
To order any of the above publications, send your name, mailing address, and the names of the publications you wish, along with a check or money order made payable to "Daedalus Publishing Company." Do not send cash. Our mailing address is Daedalus Publishing Company, 4470-107 Sunset Boulevard, Suite 375, Los Angeles, CA 90027 USA. California residents should add 8.25% sales tax. All orders should include a shipping and handling charge of $2.50 added to the total of the entire order.